Does Farting Make You Faster?

Glenn Murphy received his master's degree in science communication from London's Imperial College of Science, Technology and Medicine. He wrote his first popular science book, *Why Is Snot Green?*, while managing the Explainer team at the Science Museum in London. In 2007 he moved to the United States. He now lives and works in Raleigh, North Carolina, with his wife, Heather, and two unusually large and ill-tempered cats.

Glenn is currently writing his twelfth book.

www.glennmurphybooks.com
www.facebook.com/GlennMurphyBooks

Does Farting Make You Faster?

and other extremely important questions
(and answers) about sport
from the Science Museum

Glenn Murphy

Illustrated by Mike Phillips

MACMILLAN CHILDREN'S BOOKS

This book is produced in association with the Science Museum. Royalties from the sale of this product will help fund the museum's exhibitions and programmes.

Internationally recognized as one of the world's leading science centres, the Science Museum, London, contains more than 10,000 amazing exhibits, two fantastic simulator rides and the astounding IMAX cinema. Enter a world of discovery and achievement, where you can see, touch and experience real objects and icons which have shaped the world we live in today or visit www.sciencemuseum.org.uk to find out more.

First published 2012 by Macmillan Children's Books
a division of Macmillan Publishers Limited
20 New Wharf Road, London N1 9RR
Basingstoke and Oxford
Associated companies throughout the world
www.panmacmillan.com

ISBN 978-1-4472-1252-2

1 3 5 7 9 8 6 4 2

A CIP catalogue record for this book is available from the British Library.

Printed and bound by CPI Group (UK) Ltd, Croydon CR0 4YY

Contents

Thanks to . . .

Gaby Morgan, Steph Woolley and all at Macmillan Children's Books for their help, advice and continued support.

Holly Cave, Deborah Patterson and everyone at the Science Museum who offered comments and suggestions.

Dr David G. Haase, Professor of Physics at NC State University, for generously offering his help, suggestions and reference material.

Jennifer Jackson Weston at NC State University, for (once again) setting me up with the experts, and for very graciously ignoring a visit from President Obama to have lunch with me instead :o)

My brilliant sister (and fellow author) Lorna Murphy, whose Skype chats helped keep me sane this year.

Aaron Marco, whose physical therapy sessions helped keep me in one piece.

Brandon Sommerfeld, Martin Wheeler, Kwan Lee and Mark Jakabcsin – who all did their best to take me apart again.

Russ Campbell, Minou Pham and Scot Schwichow – all Olympians in their own way.

Chris, Susie, Heather and the Fuzzballs – big luv to you all.

And, most of all, my parents, Frank and Josephine Murphy – still sporty at well past sixty, and my daily inspiration to do better.

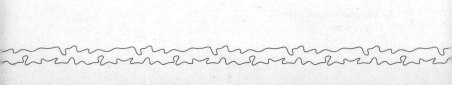

Introduction

Everybody likes sport, don't they? Well – *almost* everybody.

Do *you?*

When I was at school, all the popular kids were good at sport. They were on the **football** team, the **cricket** team, the **netball** team. I wasn't particularly good at those. But I *was* good at **swimming**, **badminton** and **fencing**.

At my university, the guys who played **rugby** and the girls who played **hockey** were the 'cool crew'. But I practised **aikido** while I studied science and nature.

I wrote this book because I love both science *and* sport, and I think they have a lot in common.

Some people (often clever, sciencey people) say they don't care much for sport. They say it's too hard, too boring or they simply can't do it. These people, I think, just haven't tried the *right sport* yet.

Other people (often sporty people) say they don't care much for science. They say it's too hard, too boring or they simply can't do it. These people, I think, just haven't read the *right science books* yet.

This book is my attempt to set 'em all straight. It's a book about sport *and* the science that lies behind it. So, hopefully, there should be something in here for *everyone*. As usual, there will be lots of **questions**, plenty of **answers** and quite a bit of **wondering** about stuff. If you've ever read one of my books before, you'll know the score* by now.

But before we kick off** here's a question for *you:*

---

* Please pardon the sporty pun.
** Sorry – I've done it again . . .

1

How far back do you think sports go? A few hundred years? A thousand years or more? Actually, sports have *always* had a role in human life.

Anthropologists (scientists who study people) and archaeologists (scientists who study old stuff) tell us that human tribes and civilizations have probably played sports for *thousands* of years – using contests of speed, strength, skill and endurance to stay healthy and prepare for battle. Many tribes still do this today – competing in everything from **footraces** and **wrestling matches** to **spear-throwing contests** and **stick-fighting competitions**.

Competitions like this have been happening throughout human history, all over the world. Some took place within villages, while others involved whole cities or countries.

Central African tribes have been competing in brutal **stick-fighting** competitions for thousands of years, travelling for miles across bushland to cross sticks with rival villages. Brutal **polo** tournaments – pitting whole villages or towns against each other in hundred-a-side games – were played in ancient Persia (now Iran) as early as the fifth century BC. The Incas and Aztecs, who built vast cities across Central and South America between the twelfth and sixteenth centuries, played a bloodthirsty ball game called **tlachtli**, which may have been invented by the Aztecs' ancestors as early as 1000 BC. In medieval **Scotland**, small villages would host their own **Highland Games**, while larger ones would host clans from all over Scotland to battle it out for the prize.

And of course, the 2,700-year-old tradition of the **Olympic Games** began in **ancient Greece**. The first was held in the city of Olympia around 776 BC. In the earliest versions of the Games, the only events were footraces like

sprints and **marathons**. But later came other events like **boxing**, **wrestling**, **javelin** and **discus throwing**.

Angry Aztec Games The ancient American Indian ball game known as tlachtli was played in huge, purpose-built arenas within Aztec and Inca cities. The tlachtli court featured a pair of stone rings at each end. Players would scramble and fight over a heavy rubber ball – much like a modern-day medicine ball – and try to plant it through the rings to score. It was like a cross between basketball, rugby and an all-out fistfight, and players often died during tlachtli games.

Scottish Olympics The Highland Games have been played in Scottish villages for at least 1,000 years. They are like a Celtic version of the Olympics, and are still held every year to this very day. Most events are centred on throwing heavy objects, such as stones, rocks and hammers. A popular event is the caber toss in which athletes lift a heavy pine pole or log up to 6.5 m in length, and toss it end-over-end for the win.

Today, sports and sporting competitions are as popular as ever, and the number of sports available to us has multiplied into the thousands, although only around thirty are played in the **Summer** and **Winter Olympics**: from track and field sports like hurdles, high jump and pole vault to team sports like football, rugby and basketball; from water sports like swimming, diving and water polo to winter sports like skiing, bobsleigh and luge; and from slow, careful games like bowling and curling to faster, crazier options like parkour, heli-skiing and freestyle BMX.

Humans are playful creatures, and most of us enjoy playing or watching some kind of sport. *Some* more than *others*, of course. There are lots of reasons why people decide they don't like a certain sport. For one thing, being human also makes us **competitive**, and *nobody* likes to lose. At least not all the time . . .

In general, though, the more you play a sport, and the more skilled you become, the more you'll enjoy it.

But how do we **get good at sport** if we're not the strongest or fastest player on the field? Are we just **born** 'brilliant at sport', or can we **learn** to be amazing athletes through practice and training? How **long** and how **hard** would you have to train to earn a spot on the England football team, a black belt in karate, or an Olympic gold medal in gymnastics?

In this book, we'll be looking at all this and more, in a high-speed race through the science of sport.

And don't worry, this isn't just a **learning** book, either. It's also a **doing** book. Along the way, you'll be **building your muscles**, **stretching your tendons** and **sharpening your reflexes**.

Do all the exercises scattered throughout this book, and you'll be running like a wolf, leaping like a leopard, swimming like a dolphin and leaving your friends in the sports-day dust. And if *that* doesn't sound like fun then I guess you'd better find a different book.

Go on, look – there's one over there, about knitting . . .

Still here? Then I guess you're up for the challenge.

Alrighty, then . . .

Ready?

Set?

Then let's **GO!**

1. Bigger, Better, Faster, Stronger

Are Olympic athletes born stronger and faster than the rest of us?

*For the most part, no. All babies are born with more or less the same bone and muscle structures. It's not really the **body you're born with** that's important – it's **what you do with it** that counts. How big, strong or fast an athlete you become will depend mostly on how you feed and train your **muscles, nerves** and **brain**.*

Is that really true?

For the most part, yes. Of course, if you suffer from a disease or growth problem, then your body may not develop quite as well, and it will be much tougher to reach the top levels of certain sports. Likewise, if you don't eat a healthy diet, or suffer from **malnutrition** (starvation or a lack of nutritious food) at a young age, then your muscles may never develop to their full size later on. But, all other things being equal, most healthy people should be able to reach Olympic levels of speed and strength with the right kind of training.

So with enough training I could run like an Olympic sprinter . . . jump like a high jumper . . . out-throw a shot putter?

Well, depending on your height, shape and body type, you may be better suited to some sports than others. The height you will eventually grow to, for example, is mostly controlled by your **genes**. So even with the best diet and training you may never be tall enough to beat high jumpers or basketball defenders a foot or more taller than you are. Likewise, if you have a long and lean body type – with narrow shoulders and thin limbs, you're unlikely to be able to out-lift a short, stocky powerlifter with a naturally powerful build. Different body types are better suited to different sports.

Sporting (Dis)abilities Until recently, it was often assumed that people with physical disabilities simply could not compete in top-level sports. But with modern training methods and technology many disabled athletes are proving this idea false. South African sprinter **Oscar Pistorius** was born without the fibula (shin) bones in both legs, and at eleven months old had to have his legs removed from just below the knee and replaced with metal prostheses (or artificial limbs). By age thirteen, he was on the school rugby team, and went on to compete in tennis, wrestling and water polo tournaments. In 2004, he took up sprinting and, fitted with new, custom-designed carbon-fibre 'cheetah' legs, he went on to win three gold medals in the 100m, 200m and 400m events at the 2008 Paralympic Athletics World Championships.

That said, there aren't that many sports – like high jump or basketball – in which height or weight are necessarily a big advantage. And with enough time and practice you can become good (if not great) at more or less any sport. Even if you're not born with the *perfect* body type for sprinting, jumping or throwing, for example, that doesn't mean you can't learn to run faster, jump higher or throw further. How far you eventually go will depend partly upon your natural shape, but mostly upon your **training**.

Sprinting, jumping and throwing, for example, are all about two things: **explosive power** and **coordination**. As far as human bodies go, these two things are taken care of by different body systems: your **musculoskeletal system**, with its network of bones, muscles and connective tissue, supplies the **power**, and your **nervous system** (including the brain) supplies the **coordination**. If you want to be an Olympic-level athlete, you have to train and develop both.

Paralympic Games Every four years, athletes affected by blindness, cerebral palsy and physical or movement disabilities compete in the Paralympic Games, held immediately after the Summer and Winter Olympics. Many have top speeds and times close to (or in some events, better than) those of able-bodied athletes. Oscar Pistorius, in particular, has since outrun many able-bodied sprinters in high-level events, coming in sixth in the 400m event of the 2005 South African Championships.

But how does that happen? I mean, aren't you more or less stuck with the body and brain you were born with?

Not at all. Muscles, bones and even entire **brains** grow,

shrink and reshape themselves throughout your life. How well they grow, and how well they work, depends mostly on what you do with them.

Most people think your bones stop growing when you reach your full adult height. But, in fact, your bones never stop growing and changing. They're constantly growing and rebuilding from the inside, and being broken down (or eaten away) from the outside. If you're ten years old, you've already re-grown your entire skeleton once. If you're over twenty, you've replaced your skeleton twice. Either way, your bones aren't the same ones you were born with!

The same goes for your muscles and nerves. Although they grow at different rates (muscles faster, nerves slower), they too can be reshaped and regrown, given the right kind of encouragement. That's where **exercise** and **training** come in.

I thought exercise was just for keeping fit, or to help you lose weight.

Done right, exercise can be a lot more than that. True, exercise can help you use up fat reserves and lose weight. And regular exercise – as we'll see later on – also helps keep your lungs and heart working properly.

But athletes do more than exercise. Athletes **train**. That means doing very special kinds of exercise, which reshape the body systems they need the most in very special ways. And they do it over and over again – day-in, day-out, throughout their sporting lives.

So how long would I have to train to be a top athlete?

Well, it varies from person to person, and from sport to

sport, so it's hard to say. Some experts reckon that *10,000 hours* of training is enough to take you from beginner to expert athlete. That seems to be the minimum for getting to a top level in most sports.

10,000 hours? So if I start now and practise for two hours a day . . .

. . . then maybe you'll become an expert in around *5,000 days*, or *thirteen and a half years*.

Nearly fourteen years?

Yep. Of course, you can become *very good* at your favourite sport with a lot less. A little sports training each week is much better than none at all, and will still make you stronger, faster, healthier and more skilled.

Most professional athletes train for several hours a day, six days a week. So, if you want to be an **Olympic champion** by the time you're twenty-five with just two hours of training a day, you need to start at age eleven!

Yikes. Better get to it, then!

No time like the present . . .

‘You're not disabled by your disabilities, you are able by your abilities.’

Oscar Pistorius,
100m, 200m, 400m gold medallist,
2008 Paralympic Games

Does your body have bits especially for doing sports?

Well, no – not quite. Your body has **systems** *for doing lots of different things, including keeping you upright, keeping you well fed and keeping you aware of your surroundings. None of these systems developed especially for doing sports. But a couple, like the* **musculoskeletal** *and* **nervous systems**, *are particularly handy for learning the physical skills needed for modern sports.*

So our bodies don't have bits just for high jumping or throwing javelins, then?

Not really, no. Jumping and throwing are both **complex skills** that involve using the brain and body together in special ways. And, while our brains and bodies *have* evolved the ability to jump and throw, this didn't happen so that we could leap over high bars or throw javelins. Instead, we developed physical abilities like this because they helped our ancestors to escape danger, hunt and **survive**.

Having a well-developed musculoskeletal and nervous system was particularly important for high-energy, physical activities like running, hunting and fighting. Later on, we turned these highly developed systems to other things.

In short, we were **born to run, hunt and fight**. But we can now use our running hunting and fighting systems to play sports too.

So what are these systems made of?

As you probably know from biology, at its most basic level, your body is made of **cells**. There are over 300 different types of cells, which do lots of *different jobs* within the body. These include red blood cells, which carry oxygen around the body; **nerve cells**, which carry messages to, from and within the brain; and **skin cells**, which help protect your body from scrapes, sunburn and nasty bacteria.

RED BLOOD CELL

OK, I get all that . . .

Now many of these cells are also organized into **tissues**. Tissues are sheets or clusters of cells that work together to perform a certain task. Again, there are lots of tissue types in the body, including **muscle tissue** (used to build your muscles), **nervous tissue** (used to build your nerves and brain) and **epithelial tissue** (used to build your skin and the lining of your gut). Most tissues contain two or more different types of cell.

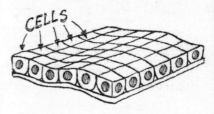

CELLS

EPITHELIAL TISSUE

Sounds simple enough.

Right. But it doesn't stop there. **Tissues**, in turn, are organized into **organs**. Just as a tissue contains two or more different cell types, an organ contains two or more types of tissue (and many, many cell types), all working together. Some organs do one job, while others do several at once. The **heart**, for example, is basically just a pump. It keeps blood moving around the body so that oxygen, carbon dioxide, sugars, hormones and other things dissolved in the bloodstream can make their way through all the body's various parts – from your lungs, liver and intestines to your brain, toes, teeth, fingers and eyeballs. The **liver**, on the other hand, does lots of different things, including filtering poisons and toxins, adding or removing sugar to your bloodstream, helping you digest fats and proteins, and much, much more.

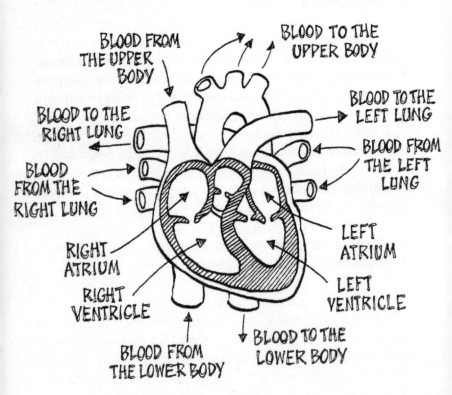

So organs are pretty important, then.

Right. They're also pretty tough to replace if they become damaged or diseased. Which is why **organ transplants** (like heart, lung or kidney transplants) are such a serious business.

But your body's amazing construction doesn't stop there – even your organs are, well . . .

. . . *organ*ized?

Exactly. Organs work together in **organ systems**. For example, your heart, veins, arteries and smaller blood vessels work together to form the **cardiovascular system**. Your teeth, stomach, liver and intestines form parts of the **digestive system**. Your kidneys and bladder are parts of the **excretory system**. And your brain, spinal cord and nerves form the **nervous system**.

All of these are important for the practice of sports and other physical activities, and we'll be coming back to them later on. But perhaps the most important of these (for sports at least) is the one that moves you about: the **musculoskeletal** system.

So how does that work?

Thought you'd never ask. Read on and let's find out . . .

Does farting make you run faster?

*Sadly, no. **Strong muscles** and **peak fitness** make you run faster, but turbocharged bottom burps will have little effect on your sprinting speed. Instead, track athletes have highly developed muscles that are built and trained for running, and powerful body systems that deliver oxygen to their muscles at a faster rate.*

You're telling me farting doesn't help at all?

Not as far as I know, no. (Although I must admit I'm not sure how hard sports scientists have tried to study that.) According to the experts, it's not **fart power** that speeds up a sprinter – it's **muscle power**.

So sprinters have *more* muscles than normal people? Like extra leg muscles or something?

Not exactly, no. Depending on how you count them, the human body contains between **206 and 250 bones**, and between **640 and 850 muscles**. And athletes have the same number of bones and muscles as everybody else.

Different muscles, then?

The difference is that champion athletes **train** their musculoskeletal systems to grow and work in different ways.

So athletes have the same *number* of muscles – they're just bigger and stronger?

Well, trained athletes do tend to have bigger, stronger muscles than your average non-sporty slob. But it's not just the size and strength of your muscles that's important. Female gymnasts, for example, are enormously strong. But they often have long, flat muscles that seem puny at first glance.

So a strong athlete *may* have bigger muscles than most people. Or they may have muscles that are longer, contain more muscle fibres or use energy and oxygen more efficiently. Through training, athletes may also gain more control over individual muscles, meaning that they can contract them harder than the average person can.

Wait – so athletes can do things with their muscles that we can't?

Sometimes, yes. As we'll see in later chapters, through training, athletes can learn to control their musculoskeletal systems to perform feats of strength, speed and agility that seem almost . . . well . . . **superhuman**.

Howzat, then?

Let's start with your standard bone-and-muscle set-up.

Your basic **musculoskeletal system** consists of a couple of hundred **bones** (arranged into a **skeleton**), along with hundreds more **muscles**, **ligaments** and **tendons**. The whole lot is wrapped in a covering of fleshy bags and straps called **connective tissue** or **fascia** (pronounced 'fash-ee-ah').

Eh? What's all that for?

It's for keeping you up. And moving you about.

But I thought your skeleton held you up. And the muscles attached to the bones move you about. You move the muscles, and the muscles pull on the bones, right?

Ah, but that's not quite the whole story. In school textbooks, you're usually shown a skeleton, and told that the hard bones give your body its shape and strength. Then the whole lot gets pulled around by stringy muscles attached to the ends of the bones. But in reality it doesn't work exactly like that.

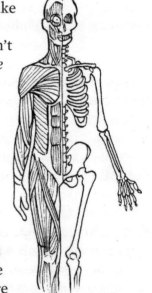

For starters, muscles don't actually attach to bones *anywhere* in the body. **Ligaments** – small, fleshy strings that don't stretch or contract very much – attach to the ends of the bones and keep them all wired together. That's what *ligament* means – 'joining thing'. But **muscles**, along with their less stretchy cousins, **tendons**, don't attach directly to bones at all. Instead, they attach to fleshy bags of **fascia** that surround every bone and every joint in your body. More layers of fascia lie outside the muscles too, wrapping round them in spiralling straps and sheets.

In fact, rather than think of a skeleton with layers of muscle, tendon and fascia on top, it's better to think of the body as a big **fleshy suit of armour**. The armour is made of fascia, and has its own strong structure. The bones and muscles float within this big suit of armour, *locked in place* by ligaments and tendons.

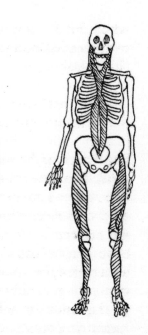

So your bones and muscles aren't the only things holding you up?

Right. *Or* the only things moving you around.

Bones, ligaments, tendons and fascia *all* give structure to the body. Together, they form **chains of pressure** around the limbs and the trunk of the body, which hold it up. But they also move you around, as the muscles within these chains change shape.

But I thought, you know, you just had one muscle on each side of every bone. Pull one muscle, and your arm moves one way. Pull the other one, and it moves the other way.

Again, that's not quite the whole story. Muscles *are* often arranged in pairs (or threes, or fours) on opposite sides of the same limb or body part. And they *do* move body parts in opposing directions. For example, shortening (or **contracting**) the **bicep muscle** (on the front of your upper arm) bends your elbow, while contracting your **tricep** (on the back of your upper arm) straightens the elbow. Similarly, contracting your **quadricep** and **hamstring** muscles – found on the front and back of your thigh – will have the effect of bending and straightening your knee.

But these muscles aren't really pulling on the arm and thigh bones to make them move. Instead, contracting your bicep muscle makes it shrink, which pulls the whole, fleshy, bony structure of the lower arm upward. The muscles pull on the tendons, the tendons on the fascia, the fascia on the bones, and the bones on everything that surrounds them. The movement may begin with a single muscle firing. But in the end the whole arm is involved in actually bending your elbow and lifting your forearm.

OK, so muscles work together with all the other stuff to move us around. So why is

that important to athletes?
Because, when they train and exercise, athletes **aren't just reshaping their muscles**. It's true that an athlete's muscles may become **longer**, **stronger** and **more efficient** than those of the average person (we'll see more about how this happens later on). But, just as importantly, athletes also reshape their **tendons**, **fascia** – even their **bones** – to adjust to new, powerful and sporty movements.

So it's not that top athletes have *more* muscles than everyday people – they have the *same* number of muscles as everybody else. It's what's inside them – and all around them – that's different.

OK . . . so *how* different can they get?
Let's find out . . .

Sprints, Hurdles and Relays

Could the world's fastest sprinter beat a cheetah?

Not a chance. A **cheetah** *can hit around 70mph (112km/h), which makes them more than twice as speedy as the world's fastest human sprinters, who have yet to top 28mph (45km/h). Even your pet cat could beat that.*

What?! My cat could outrun an Olympic sprinter?! No way!

Yep. I'm afraid so. The average moggy can easily hit 30 mph (48km/h) at a full sprint. This makes them a little faster than 100m-sprint world-record holder **Usain Bolt**, whose fastest speed in his record-breaking 2009 race was just under 27.8mph (45km/h).

Bigger cats, like lions and leopards, can sprint at over 50 mph (80km/h), and would leave all human sprinters in the dust. As for racing a cheetah – forget about it. In 2009, **Usain Bolt** made history by running the 100m sprint in just 9.58 seconds. In theory, a cheetah could do it in less than four seconds.

In tests, even lazy cheetahs, coaxed into chasing stuffed toys (dragged from cars by curious scientists), have run 100m in under 6.5 seconds.

By the time Usain Bolt hit the finish line, the cheetah would already be sitting there, licking its paws.

Are cats especially fast sprinters, then?

Cats are fast, but not uniquely so. As a matter of fact, though, *plenty* of mammals can outrun us over short distances, including **warthogs** (30mph), **grizzly bears** (30mph) and **giraffes** (32mph). Which just goes to show . . .

. . . that you should never try to outrun a grizzly bear?

Well, yes. But, also, humans *aren't really built for sprinting*. We're very good at long-distance running (more about that later). And some of us are *much* faster than others. But, compared to other mammals, we have a pretty feeble top speed.

Why is that?

It's partly to do with how our muscles are built, or, more specifically, the type and number of **muscle fibres** within them.

There are three types of muscle in the human body – **skeletal muscle** (which covers and surrounds the skeleton), **smooth muscle** (which covers and lines the internal organs) and **cardiac muscle** (found only in the heart). We're really only interested in skeletal muscle, here, since this is the one that gives us our strength, speed and agility in sports.

Sprinting

How to play
An athletic sport in which runners compete head-to-head, trying to cover short distances in the shortest time possible. The most famous and popular sprint race is the 100m sprint, but others include the shorter 60m dash and the longer 200m and 400m races.

Players
One – sprinters compete individually against up to nine rival athletes in their own track lanes.

Equipment
Shoes – lightweight leather/plastic running shoes moulded to the athlete's foot, with metal spikes in the bottom to grip the running track.

Rules
Each runner is assigned his/her own lane, in which they must stay throughout the race, and begins the race in a crouch – both feet placed on special, track-mounted starting blocks. At the starter's signal, the race is on. The winner is the first to cross the finish line.

Muscle fibres are tiny, fleshy threads that are bundled together to create whole muscles like the biceps or triceps. Now here's the tricky bit. There are two kinds of skeletal muscle fibre: **type I** (or **slow-twitch**) and **type II** (**fast-twitch**).

Type I muscle fibres need oxygen to generate energy and turn it into movement. They *can take a lot of strain*, and as long as they're well supplied with oxygen and sugar they *take a long time to tire*.

Type II fibres *do not need oxygen* to create energy. They have their own fuel stores, which they start burning immediately to generate *quick, powerful bursts of strength and speed*.

So which one do you think you find more of in sprinters?

Err . . . the second one?

Right. Most human muscles contain *both* types of fibres. The amount of fast-twitch fibres in muscles varies. But, in Olympic sprinters, up to 80% of the leg and hip muscles consist of type II (fast-twitch) fibres. This is part of what makes Usain Bolt way faster than average. Elite sprinters train to increase the amount of fast-twitch fibres in their muscles.

So they can be more like cheetahs?

Something like that, yes.

So how much fast-twitch muscle does a cheetah have?

Good question. In a cheetah, it's more like *82%* fast-twitch muscle. This may not seem like *that* much more. But combined with the cheetah's longer, four-legged stride (and some other neat tricks it has for sprinting) this makes the cheetah, in turn, more than *twice* as fast as Usain Bolt.

Do you think, one day, a human sprinter *will* come along who can outrun a cheetah?

It seems unlikely. Experts reckon that even with as much fast-twitch muscle as possible, human beings are incapable of reaching more than **30 to 35mph**. With the right diet and training, you *can* alter your muscle structure, increase your running speed by 50% or more and maybe even become an Olympic champion. But, no matter what-a you eat-a . . .

. . . you won't-a beat a cheetah?

Exactly.

I'm going to write that on my running vest.

Animals that Can Out-sprint Humans

Top Speed (mph)	Animal
27.8	human (Usain Bolt)
30	warthog, grizzly bear, kangaroo, domestic cat
32	reindeer, giraffe
35	rabbit, jackal
40	greyhound, zebra, ostrich, hyena
50	lion, wildebeest
70	cheetah

Why do hurdlers do the splits when they jump?

Unlike long jumpers, hurdlers try not to spend too much time in the air. Their split-legged leaps allow them to clear hurdles quickly and, quite literally, hit the ground running when they land.

How does jumping with one foot forward help with all that?
What do you mean?

Why don't they just, you know, do a super-long jump over each hurdle — throwing both feet forward, like a long-jumper?
OK, how would that help?

Well, they'd cover more distance with each jump, so they wouldn't have to run so much in between.
Let's think about that for a minute. In a standard 110m hurdles race, the runners have to cover the distance as quickly as possible, clearing ten hip-height hurdles along the way. Agreed?

Agreed.
Now which do you think takes more effort – leaping a 1.2m hurdle, or running a few metres along the flat track?

Dunno.

Let me put it this way. Which would you rather do: run once round an athletics track, or work your way round the same track in a series of non-stop hip-height leaps, one right after another?

Yikes. I'd rather run. I don't know if I'd even *make it* once round the track doing non-stop jumps like that.
Me neither.

So leaping takes more effort than running?
Right. To leap over a high hurdle, you have to generate a pretty large amount of force with your jumping leg, just to overcome the effects of gravity pulling down on your body. And the heavier you are the harder you have to contract your leg muscles to achieve lift-off.

Running, by comparison, is easy. Sprinting also requires powerful contractions of your thigh and calf muscles, one leg right after the other. But it takes less force to shift your weight one metre *horizontally* along the track than it does to shift it one metre *vertically*, or straight up. It's like the difference between driving a car (horizontal movement) and launching a rocket (vertical movement).

OK — that makes sense, I s'pose.
This is one reason why hurdlers spend more time running than leaping. Tough as it is, sprinting takes less energy.

Now, what if I asked you to race a friend round the same track, only you're allowed to *run the whole way*, while your friend has to do the *non-stop, bounding leaps* we talked about before. Who do you think would cross the finish line first?

Hurdling

How to play
An athletic sport in which runners compete head-to-head, trying to cover a short or middle distance as quickly as possible – leaping over ten hip-height obstacles as they go. The event combines sprinting and leaping, requiring agility and timing as well as speed. Hurdles races are run over short (100m for women, 110m for men) and middle (400m) distances.

Players
One – hurdlers compete individually, against up to nine rival athletes in their own track lanes.

Equipment
Shoes – leather/plastic running shoes with spikes, like those used in sprinting.

Hurdles – gate-like obstacles consisting of a wooden crossbar mounted on a 1.2m-high metal stand. 400m races feature **low hurdles**, measuring 0.7m high for women, and 0.9m for men. 100m and 110m races feature **high hurdles** – 0.84m high for women, 1m high for men.

Rules
As in sprinting, each runner is assigned his/her own lane, in which they must stay throughout the race, and begins the race on starting blocks. At the starter's signal, the race is on. All ten hurdles must be cleared. There is no penalty for knocking them over, but this obviously slows the runners down, so they try not to do so. The winner is the first to cross the finish line.

Wait — is my friend a kangaroo?

Err . . . no. Your friend is human. Like you.

Oh. OK. In that case, it's just stupid. I would win easily, because it wouldn't be a fair race.

Why not?

Because running is much faster than — ohhhhhhhh, now I get it . . .

Exactly. The runner would cover the same ground much faster than the jumper. That's because the more time you spend in the air, the less time you can spend **accelerating**.

Runners accelerate (or speed up) a little bit every time a foot pushes off the ground. But, the second the foot leaves the ground and stops pushing, **drag** – caused by **air resistance** – starts to slow the runner down in mid-air.

Sprinters maintain top speed by taking lots of short, rapid strides, spending as little time 'in the air' as possible, to avoid losing speed. Hurdlers try their best to do the same. They do so by (a) *jumping just high enough* to clear each hurdle, (b) *spending as little time as possible in the air* and (c) *resuming their sprint as soon as possible* after landing. The split-legged, one-foot-forward leap of the hurdler helps them to do all three of these things. *That's* why they do it.

In fact, top hurdlers spend almost as much time perfecting their leaping technique as they do exercising and running. Like sprinters, hurdlers train hard to *build lots of fast-twitch muscle fibre* in their leg muscles. But they also *stretch* the muscles and tendons of their legs to make them more flexible, and do special **plyometric exercises** to build explosive power for leaping.

We'll learn more about this type of exercise later. But if you want to give this a go right now – and add rocket-like leaping power to your legs – then follow the instructions below.

Give it a go!

Exercise: jump squat
Type: plyometric
Goal: leg strength, explosive power for leaping and jumping

Start standing, both feet flat on the ground, hip-width apart. Place your hands either side of your head, palms facing forward, fingers to temples. Keeping your back straight, quickly squat down, lowering your hips to your heels immediately. Push back up, straightening both legs and launching yourself off the ground in a standing position. Land toes first, and repeat.

Try to do as many as you can in one minute. Here's what you should aim for:

up to 10/min	beginner
10–20/min	intermediate
20–30/min	athlete
30–50/min	champion

Relay Racing

How to play

An athletic sport in which groups of four runners take turns running parts of the same race, passing a metal baton between them as they go. The winning team is the one whose final runner passes the finish line first, with the baton still in hand. Relays are run over a range of distances from short (4 x 100m, 4 x 200m) to middle (4 x 400m, 4 x 800m, 4 x 1,600m).

Players

Teams of four runners compete against each other. All relay events are run in four parts or 'legs', with one team member taking each leg.

Equipment

Shoes – leather/plastic running shoes with spikes, like those used in sprinting.

Baton – a simple 30cm aluminium tube. Smooth and lightweight, this is easily dropped by sweaty hands, so runners must take care during handovers.

Rules

Each team is assigned their own lane, and the four runners on each team are staggered at equal distances round the track. The first runner of each team holds the baton, and at the starter's signal sets off from the starting line. At each changeover (or hand-off) point, the runners have a distance of 20m to exchange the baton. The receiver sets off when he sees his teammate behind him, and extends a hand behind himself in mid-run, into which his teammate places the baton. The final runner for each team is called the anchor. The winning team is the one whose anchor crosses the finish line – baton in hand – first.

Jumps and Pole Vaulting

What's the highest, and furthest, a human has ever jumped?

*As of 2012, the **highest** an athlete has ever jumped in a sporting competition is **2.45m**. The **longest** jump, a record dating way back to 1991, is **8.95m**.*

Under 2.5m? Is that it? That doesn't seem so high.

Why do you say that?

Well, since most high jumpers are over six feet tall, about two metres, anyway, that means they only have to jump half a metre, doesn't it?

If all they had to do was touch the bar with their *heads*, then yes. But in a high-jump event, you have to get your *whole body* over the bar – head, hips, feet, the lot. Imagine a brick wall, the top of which is *at least a metre higher than your own head*. Now imagine trying to jump right over it, in one go, without grabbing (or even touching) the top.

Oh. I didn't think of it like that.

Yep. And champion high-jump athletes do that every day.

So why do they jump over it *backwards*, then? That's always seemed a bit silly to me.

The modern high jumper's backward-flopping leap is

called the **Fosbury Flop**, named after American high jumper **Dick Fosbury**. He invented the technique in 1963, when he was just sixteen years old. After he used it to win a gold medal for America in the 1968 Olympic Games – setting a new world record with a jump of 2.24m – other jumpers began using his strange, back-first method. Within ten years, *every* Olympic athlete was jumping that way.

So how did they *used* to jump? Like, before this Fosbury dude? Did they just run up to it and jump straight up?

Nope. Before Fosbury, most high jumpers jumped *sideways*, using one of two methods.

Sideways? But why?

If you think about it, this makes perfect sense. However you decide to jump, your feet are the *lowest points* of your body, the *last things* to leave the ground, and the *hardest things* to get over the bar.

With that in mind, you can see how facing the bar and jumping forward (as they did in the Olympics of ancient Greece) will only get you so high.

Why's that?

Well, let's say you manage a mighty leap that *lifts your hips 1.8m* off the ground, higher than your own head height. No matter how tightly you tuck your feet up, they'll still be a few centimetres lower than your hips as you fly through the air. So the lowest points of your body (your feet) never get more than about 1.7m off the ground, and that's the highest you'll ever be able to jump using this method.

High Jump

How to play
An athletic sport in which athletes leap – backwards and belly-up – over a high horizontal bar, landing safely on a thick, foam-and-plastic 'crash mat'. After each jump, the bar is raised. The winner is the athlete who clears the bar at the highest level.

Players
One – high jumpers compete individually, taking turns to make jumps.

Equipment
Shoes – spiked leather/plastic shoes, like those used by sprinters but with thicker soles for greater stability.
Jump bar – aluminium or plastic bar 4m in length, balanced upon a tall metal stand. The bar can be set at any height from 1–3m.*

Rules
The athlete runs towards the jump bar at an angle, and takes off one-footed from the ground before it. For the jump to qualify, the athlete must clear the bar without knocking it loose from the stand. Each jumper gets three attempts. The jumper who clears the bar at the highest setting wins the competition.

---

* In fact, high-jump bars used to only go up to 2.4m. But, when the men's high-jump record topped 2.45m in 1993, they had to start building them taller!

Even very tall athletes couldn't hope to clear more than two metres this way.

In fact, in the entire history of Olympic high jump, no one managed to clear the two-metre mark until after 1900, when two new sideways-jumping methods – the **scissors jump** and the **western roll** – began to appear.

So what do *they* look like?

To perform a **scissors jump**, the athlete runs at the bar at an angle, jumps *forward and sideways* with the chest and head upright, and swoops one straight leg – followed by the other – over the bar, in a kind of *scissor-kicking motion*. This lifts the feet (however temporarily) above hip level, increasing the maximum height of the jump.

In a **western roll** (also known as the **parallel straddle jump**), the athlete jumps sideways and flies – chest down and starfish-like – over the bar, 'rolling' over the top of it in mid-air. Flattening the body like this lifts the feet up to hip level, making it easier to get them over the bar.

Using these methods, high jumpers managed to clear the two-metre mark for the first time in history, and went on setting new records with them until 1968, when the **Fosbury Flop** came along.

In a Fosbury Flop, the athlete leaps backwards, leading with the back of the head, and arches his/her body over the bar. First the head, then the shoulder blades, hips, backs of the knees and finally the heels clear the bar one by one. The jumper lands flat on his/her back, usually finishing with a backwards roll as the legs continue swinging over the face.

*‘I didn't train to make the Olympic team until 1968.
I simply trained for the moment. I never even imagined I
would be an Olympic athlete. It always seemed to evolve.’*

Dick Fosbury,
Olympic high jumper, gold medallist,
and President of the World Olympians Association

This turned out to be the most efficient way anyone has ever found (at least so far) of lifting your **centre of gravity** (hips), along with the head, feet and everything else, over the greatest possible height. That's why Olympic high jumpers still use it today to break records, clearing heights of 2.4m or more.

So jumping *backwards* turned out to be the best way. That's pretty crazy.
Yep.

What about long jumpers, then? Why do they jump feet first, rather than head first? Is that so they can jump higher too?
Well, yes and no. For long jumpers, the goal is a bit different. In high jump, the athlete is trying to turn as much of the energy of the run-up as possible into vertical motion, to get as high as possible. But in long jump height isn't as important as maintaining speed.

Long jumpers are basically sprinters who try to *keep as much of their horizontal footspeed and momentum as possible* during a last-minute leap into the air. Once they've left the ground, throwing both feet forward helps to keep their centre of gravity moving *along*, rather than

Long Jump

How to play
An athletic sport in which athletes take a running leap into a long sandpit, trying to cover the greatest possible distance before a feet-first landing.

Players
One – long-jumpers compete individually, taking turns to make jumps.

Equipment
Shoes – spiked leather/plastic shoes, like those used by sprinters.
Jump pit – a sand-filled pit 2.7m wide, and more than 9m long. Before it lies a long **run-up track** with a narrow, wooden **take-off board** set into it 1m from the pit.

Rules
The athlete runs as fast as possible, and takes off one-footed from the wooden take-off board. Stepping past a line – marked with soft putty – on the take-off board results in a fault, and the jump is disqualified. Once landed, the distance is measured from the forward edge of the take-off board to the rearmost impression left by the jumper in the sandpit. Each jumper gets three attempts. The longest cleared distance wins the competition.

upward. Some long jumpers also continue their 'run' in mid-air, with a cycling motion of the legs. This, too, helps keep their weight moving forward.

Reaching out with the feet also helps prevent the jumper from falling backwards into the sand at the end of the jump. Since the total jump distance is measured to the rearmost 'dent' they leave in the sand, falling back after a jump is a catastrophic mistake.

Using this feet-first-flying method, male long jumpers have cleared distances of almost **9m**, while triple jumpers have managed an impressive **18.3m**.

Wait — triple jumpers can jump further than long jumpers?

Well, in triple jump, the take-off board from which the jump is measured is set *12m further back* from the landing pit. It's from here that the triple jumper begins his first leap, making *two more* leaping, bounding steps before leaving the ground for the last time, sailing through the air and landing in the sandpit. Since they count the bit where they're hopping and skipping as part of the jump, triple jumpers naturally cover more ground than long jumpers.

Hey — that's cheating!

But still, even subtracting the extra 'skipping distance' they're allowed, that would make their record stand at around **6.3m** by long-jump standards. That's about the length of a half-sized swimming pool, or two-thirds the length of an average London bus. Not bad at all, considering they have to *skip* their way through most of the run-up!

Wow. I don't think I could jump that far, no matter how I did it!

If you want to add some length to your own jumps, try these simple exercises. Practice makes perfect!

Give it a go!

Exercise: standing long jump
Type: plyometric/skill
Goal: explosive power, coordination

1. Stand at a marked point on the ground or grass, with both feet flat on the ground, hip-width apart. Start with your arms held straight behind you.
2. Bend your knees, swing your arms forward and jump as far as you can along the ground landing on the balls of both feet, with good balance.
3. Turn round, and see if you can jump back on to your original take-off spot.
4. Turn round and repeat the jump – this time trying to beat your previous record. Use a tape measure to record your personal best each week.
5. Find a couple of friends, and stage a standing jump competition.

The world record for a standing long jump is **3.71m**. Good luck!

Triple Jump

How to play

An athletic sport in which athletes take a hopping, skipping leap into a long sandpit, trying to cover the greatest possible distance before a feet-first landing.

Players

One – triple jumpers compete individually, taking turns to make jumps.

Equipment

Shoes – spiked leather/plastic shoes, like those used by sprinters.

Jump pit – a sand-filled pit identical to that used in long jump, except that the wooden take-off board is set 11–13m back from the pit.

Rules

As in long jump, athletes must begin their jumps from a take-off board set back from the sandpit, and crossing the marked line on the board results in a disqualified jump. After the initial **'hopping'** take-off, the jumper must land *on the same* foot he/she took off with for the second **'skipping' jump**. For the third and final **stepping jump**, the jumper must switch feet – taking off from the opposite foot to that of the previous, hopping jump. Both legs must come in front of the athlete as they land.

Judges measure the distance from the take-off point to the first mark the athlete leaves in the sand.

How do you learn to pole vault (without seriously injuring yourself)?

Pole vaulting is probably the most difficult to learn of all the athletic field skills. To do it well, you need great strength, timing and coordination. But you learn to do it the same way you learn any other physical skill: little by little, by trial and error, until your brain and body commit the movement to memory.

I'm not surprised it's the most difficult. I mean, pole vaulting *looks* hard.

Yep. No two ways about it: pole vaulting *is* hard.

To pull off a successful pole vault, you have to do *all* the following things, and all with *perfect timing*:

1. **Run** at close to full speed, carrying a pole up to 5m long over your head.
2. Without stopping, **plant** the tip of the pole precisely into a box just 15cm wide and 20cm deep.
3. **Leap** into the air, **hang on** to the pole as it bends almost in two, and **swing your legs** towards the sky until you're in a perfect upside-down handstand on the end of the upright pole.
4. **Flip** your whole body over the high bar without knocking into it (or letting your pole knock into it).
5. **Fall** feet first 5–6m, back to earth, landing squarely on the crash mat without hurting yourself.

To do all this perfectly, you must have great coordination. That means spending weeks, months and years training your brain to fire *precisely the right muscle groups* at *exactly the right times*.

We'll be learning a bit more about how this happens in chapter 4. But for now just understand this: learning any physical skill as complex as pole vaulting takes a bit of *knowledge*, a lot of *coaching*, tons of *practice* and the formation of something called **muscle memory**.

Once a skill has been performed, corrected and repeated enough times, your body learns how to do it without thinking, and it'll remember how to do it for many years afterwards. All skills that enter your muscle memory are like this. Remember when you first learned to ride a bike?

Yeah. That was hard too.

Right. It was tricky at first, but with enough practice you could do it if you concentrated on pedalling steadily, keeping your balance and not falling off. But after a bit more practice you didn't need to think about pedalling or balancing at all. The bike-riding skill entered your muscle memory, and you gained the ability to ride a bike without thinking.

That's all very well, but it's not quite the same with pole vaulting, is it?
Why's that?

I mean, if you fall off a bike, you just topple to the ground. If you fall off a pole in mid-vault, you could end up falling five metres on to your head!
Very true.

So how do you learn to do something that difficult and dangerous without crippling yourself or cracking your head open or something?!
You take it a little at a time, making sure your body is happy with each 'baby step' along the way. Here's how most beginners build up to a full pole vault in ten small, safe steps.

1. Practise **jogging** and **running** with the pole over your head.
2. Practise **dipping** the end of the pole towards the ground as you run.
3. Practise small **leaps** off the ground, right after the tip of the pole touches the ground.
4. Practise **planting** the pole into the pole box in mid-jog, but don't jump.
5. Hold the pole halfway down (to limit the height), then practise **mini-vaults**. To do these, you jog at the box, plant the pole, make a small jump and **hang on to the pole** (head up, feet down) as you ride it the short distance to the crash mat, landing feet first.

6. Repeat the mini-vault, this time **lifting both feet** to make an L-shape, so that you cling to the pole in a seated position, landing on your bottom.
7. Repeat, but this time **swing your feet higher**, pointing them towards the sky. Land on your back.
8. Repeat, swinging your feet up and extending your hips and arms until you're fully **inverted** (upside down). Turn in the air and land chest down, facing back the way you came.
9. Now grip the pole a bit higher and try the same, this time letting the pole bend a little before you swing your feet up, and **do a full half-twist** in the air, landing on your feet.
10. Grip the end of the pole, and go for a **full pole vault**, sticking to a low height for the bar at first.

Do all that, slowly, carefully, and with the help of a qualified coach, and you'll be doing your first proper pole vault within weeks. Then it takes many more months (or years) to get *really* good at it.

Blimey. Seems like a lot of hard work.
Well, you could always take up long jump instead. Or move to Eastern Europe.

How would that help?
I hear they're very good at pole vaulting in Pole-land!

[Groan]
Heheheheh.

'You need to work very hard; you have to spend a lot of time practising your sport – six to seven hours daily.'

Sergey Bubka,
Olympic pole-vault gold medallist,
who broke the world record for pole vaulting *35 times*

Pole Vault

How to play
An athletic sport in which athletes use a long, flexible fibreglass pole to launch themselves over an incredibly high horizontal bar, landing safely on a foam and plastic crash mat on the other side.

Players
1 – pole vaulters compete individually, taking turns to make jumps.

Equipment
Pole – fibreglass or carbon-fibre pole measuring anywhere from 3–5m in length, with adjustable handgrips.
High bar – like a high-jump bar, only adjustable to 6m or more. Beneath the bar, there's also a small metal-sided **pole box** dug into the track, measuring 1m long, 15cm wide and sloping down to a depth of 20cm.

Rules
As in high jump, pole vaulters get three attempts at clearing a chosen height. Athletes take turns to try the same height. When two or more vaulters successfully clear the bar at a given height, the bar is raised. The competition continues until one vaulter is left. If it gets down to two vaulters, and they both fail to make the final height, then there may be a sudden-death 'jump-off' to decide the winner.

Javelin, Discus, Shot Put and Hammer Throws

Has anyone ever lobbed a discus right out of a stadium?

*According to legend, the Greek hero **Heracles** (the Romans called him Hercules) once did this in one of the first ever Olympic Games. But in reality the discus thrown in modern athletic events is too heavy to be thrown that far. Throwing the discus, javelin, shot put or hammer any sort of distance takes a lot of strength and a great deal of training.*

Come on, how hard could it be? I lobbed a frisbee right out of our local park once. And I'm no Olympic athlete.

OK . . . but frisbees are usually made of plastic, and they're very light. Most only weigh 200g or less.

So how heavy *is* a discus, then?

Between **1–2kg**, or about the weight of a good-sized bag of potatoes. They're made of heavy rubber and metal, and they're about the same size as a small dinner plate, only much thicker in the middle. But imagine hurling the bag of potatoes – rather than the dinner plate – and you'll have a better idea of how far it's likely to go.

Yeah, I doubt I could've thrown those spuds over the trees, right enough. So what about javelins, hammers and stuff?

At between **600g and 800g**, an Olympic **javelin** weighs about the same as a discus. The solid-metal **hammers** and **shots** used in hammer throw and shot put are quite a bit heavier, weighing up to 7.2kg.

What exactly are hammers and shots, anyway?

The **shot** is a solid metal ball, usually made of iron and steel. The **hammer** is a metal ball on the end of a long metal chain with a handle at one end for swinging. The shot gets its name from the weighty **cannonballs** (also known as **iron shots**) that were thrown in older versions of the event. 'Shot putting', then, is literally putting the shot as far away from yourself as possible in a single toss.

Similarly, ancient **hammer-throwing** events used to be just that – throwing large, heavy **blacksmith's hammers**. At some point, the objects used for the official games changed, but the names stuck. In any case, you can see why no one (except the legendary Heracles – and he was supposed to be half Greek god!) has managed to throw these things right out of a stadium. We may not throw real cannonballs or hammers any more, but their modern equivalents are no easier to fling that sort of height and distance.

For this reason, athletes who compete in these field events train long and hard for many years to improve their throwing ability.

Discus Throw

How to play
An athletic sport in which athletes make spinning throws to launch a heavy disc as far as possible into a cone-shaped outdoor target area. The discus must land within the target area to score, and the athlete with the longest qualifying throw wins the game.

Players
One – discus throwers compete individually, taking turns to make throws.

Equipment
Discus – heavy, plate-like disc made mostly of rubber, with a metal core and edge for extra weight. Parts of it can also be made from plastic, wood, fibreglass or carbon fibre. In international competitions, the men's discus weighs 2kg, and measures 22cm across. The discus used in the women's event weighs 1kg, and is around 18cm across.
Target – a cone-shaped grass (or synthetic grass) pitch with a 2.5m clay circle where the athlete stands and spins before their throw. Since the spinning athlete could accidentally launch the discus backwards during a bad throw, the back of the throwing circle is surrounded by a tall, U-shaped cage.

Rules
Athletes take turns to throw for a maximum of three attempts. Stepping out of the front of the throwing circle results in a disqualified throw. At the end of three throws, the thrower who has managed the longest distance with a single throw wins.

But can you really get *that* much better at throwing heavy things, even with practice? I mean, only huge, muscle-bound athletes throw javelins and hammers and stuff. Isn't it just the biggest and strongest athletes who throw the furthest?

Not necessarily. Just because an athlete is big and muscly doesn't mean he's stronger than his smaller rivals. And, even if he is strong, that doesn't automatically mean he has the *explosive strength* and *technique* needed for a world-class throw.

What do you mean?

Well, we've already learned that **explosive power** comes from **quick-firing (fast-twitch) muscle fibres**, and that success in sprinting and jumping requires plenty of these fibres in the muscles of the legs and hips, right?

Right.

Well, throwing a javelin, discus or shot put requires massive amounts of explosive power too. This comes from exercising the muscles of the upper body (the arms, chest and back, in particular) in ways that increase the number of **fast-twitch fibres** within.

You can make your muscles grow bigger by *lifting heavy weights very slowly* (bodybuilders and weightlifters do this all the time). When you do this, you're actually making tiny rips in your muscle fibres. Later, as you rest and recover from training, your body repairs your torn muscle fibres, just in case you try the same thing again. As a result, your muscles grow stronger.

Now, this type of slow strength training *will* make

you better at lifting weights, and may also increase your **maximum strength** – or the maximum total weight you're able to lift. But that *won't* necessarily make you better at throwing a javelin or shot.

Why not?
Because **explosive movements** like throwing demand *much* more power than lifting your maximum load. Just because you can *lift* a 100kg object off the ground doesn't mean you can *throw* it. In fact, you'd almost certainly injure yourself trying. If you want the sort of power you need for Olympic throwing events, building big arm muscles is not enough. You also have to build muscles that can *contract harder and faster*, giving more *explosive bursts of power* to your arms, legs and core muscles.

So how do you do that?
You start by lifting weights slowly to build your muscles to increase your **maximal strength**, then continue by using special types of exercise to *convert* that maximal strength into **explosive power**. For the most part, this means using something called **plyometrics**.

In plyometric exercise, you begin by *lengthening* a muscle, then force it to *contract hard and fast*, then *immediately* force it to *stretch out* again, and *repeat*. You can do this using weights, or with bodyweight exercises like the **plyometric press-up** (see page 52 if you want to give it a go yourself).

Javelin Throw

How to play

An athletic sport in which athletes run and throw a sharp-ended metal pole as far as possible into a cone-shaped, outdoor target area.

Players

One – javelin throwers compete individually, taking turns to make throws.

Equipment

Javelin – thin metal pole tapered at both ends, with a sharp metal tip. Men's javelins weigh around 1kg, and are around 2.7m long. Women's javelins weigh around 0.6kg, and measure around 2.3m in length.

Target – a cone-shaped grass (or synthetic grass) pitch around 100m long, fanning out to cover a 30° area. In front of it is a short, clay-surfaced run-up track with a wooden stop board, similar to the take-off boards used in long jump.

Rules

Athletes take turns to throw for a maximum of three attempts. Stepping or hopping over the throwing line results in a disqualified throw. The javelin must land tip-down to score – flat bounces do not count. After three throws, the thrower who has managed the longest distance with a single throw wins.

Give it a go!

Exercise: press-up
Type: plyometric
Goal: arm strength, explosive power for throwing

1. Start lying face down on the ground, palms either side of your chest.
2. Keeping your back and legs straight, you're going to push down hard with your hands, straightening your elbows and launching your body off the ground. Throughout this movement, you should stay straight from the backs of your heels to the back of your neck, as if you have a long plank attached to your spine and the backs of your legs.
3. For a standard press-up, all you have to do is straighten your elbows. But for a plyometric press-up you have to push hard enough to lift your hands right off the ground, so that you're lifted – straight-backed and straight-armed – into the air. Clap your hands together while you're in the air.
4. As you drop back down, let your elbows bend to absorb and slow your fall, lowering your chest to within a few centimetres of the ground.
5. Repeat.

Try to do as many as you can in a minute. Here's what you should aim for:

up to 10/min	beginner
10–20/min	intermediate
20–30/min	athlete
30–50/min	superathlete

As with all muscle-building exercise, this creates miniature snaps and tears in your muscle fibres, which grow back stronger as they heal. But it also encourages the growth of **fast-twitch muscle fibres**, specifically, which grow back much thicker and stronger than they were before.

In practice, most throwers *do* end up pretty huge. They tend to have very large chest, arm and back muscles, and develop huge maximum *and* explosive strength. But it's not just the size of the muscles – it's what's inside them – that counts.

OK, so now you're super-strong, and you have crazy exploding chest muscles. Now you're ready to win the gold medal for discus?

Nope. Not by a long shot.

What? Why not?

Because to be good at the throwing events you have to study and practise correct **throwing technique**. After all, it's no use being ultra-strong and having all that explosive muscle-power if you end up tossing a discus or hammer in the wrong direction. Any throw that fails to land in the target field will be disqualified – even if it travels a record-breaking distance. Throwing hard *and* throwing in the right direction can be tricky. And it's trickier in some events than others.

Shot Put

How to play

An athletic sport in which athletes throw, or 'put', a very heavy metal ball (called the **shot**) as far as possible into a cone-shaped outdoor target area. Athletes throw the shot from their neck, keeping it above shoulder height, in an outward pushing motion.

Players

One – shot putters compete individually, taking turns to make throws.

Equipment

Shot – solid metal ball, usually made of iron, steel, brass or tungsten. Sizes vary, but the minimum weight for men's events is 7.4kg; for women's events, it is 4kg.

Target – a cone-shaped grass (or synthetic grass) pitch similar to that used in discus, but just 30m long, and fanning out over a slightly wider, 35° area. But since shot putters don't spin much during throws,* there is no safety cage round the rear of the throwing circle.

Rules

Athletes take turns to throw for a maximum of three attempts. Stepping out of the front of the throwing circle results in a disqualified throw. The shot must land within the target area to score and, as in discus and javelin, the athlete with the longest qualifying throw after three throws wins the game.

---

* And the heavy shot can't travel far, anyway.

Shot put, for example, is pretty straightforward. You just hold the shot next to your chin, hop across the throwing circle, pivot and launch the shot as far as possible. Javelin is a little harder, as you have to try to transfer the energy from the run-up into a perfect straight, high-angled throw. But throwing the discus the correct way is *much* harder.

Really? That hard? But isn't it just like tossing a heavy frisbee?

Nope. As we've already learned, the discus is *much* heavier than a frisbee. So, to throw it any sort of distance, you can't get away with a quick flick of the wrist or elbow. In fact, you have to use the strength and power of your whole body, combined with a spinning motion that transfers your weight (or, rather, **momentum**) to the flying disc.

So how do they do it?

Discus throwers start facing away from the throwing field, holding the discus in one downturned palm. To start the throw, they step and spin their bodies through 540° (one and a half turns), crossing the throwing circle as they do so. Taking care not to step out of the throwing circle, they end the spin facing the target field, finally releasing the discus from the little-finger side of the palm, sending it spinning into the air.

Hammer throwers use **spin** to add speed to their throws, too, in an even trickier motion. They hold the handle of the hammer's chain with both hands, start the hammer swinging over their heads, then sit back into the hips as they spin right round *three or four times* before releasing the handle of the hammer and letting it fly into the air. As in discus, the spinning generates an **angular** (or circular)

momentum of the thrower and his hammer, which is transferred into the **linear** (straight-line) **momentum** of the hammer as it flies free.

Whoa. That sounds kind of dangerous. Hasn't anyone ever . . . you know . . . turned three and a half times and launched the hammer towards the crowd?

That does happen, yes. And wildly thrown hammers *do* still injure people from time to time. In the past, quite a few people (mostly coaches and trainers standing close to the thrower) have even been *killed* this way.

Yikes!

But nowadays the **throwing circle** used in the hammer-throw event is surrounded by a **tall, C-shaped cage**, which protects the coaches and crowds alike from heavy iron hammers released too soon, or too late.

That's a relief. In that case, I might actually watch it some time.

Well, it's always safe if you're watching it on TV . . .

'It took me time to realize that the men who won Olympic gold medals in the decathlon are just men, just like me.'

Dan O'Brien,
Olympic decathlete and gold medallist

Give it a go!

Exercise: stick javelin
Type: skill
Goal: skill, coordination

1. Find a lightweight stick (e.g. thin bamboo cane of the type used to hold up plants), and a wide, open space with plenty of room to throw (and no one to injure).
2. Mark a line on the ground or grass, and stand a few metres back from it, holding the stick in one hand, about halfway along its length.
3. Lift the stick until it's parallel to the ground and alongside your ear.
4. Jog at the line and, before you reach it, angle the tip of the stick upwards at about 45°.
5. Plant the opposite foot (to the hand holding the stick) on the ground before you reach the line, and launch the stick into the air, tip-first.
6. Note where it lands. Repeat the throw, experimenting with different angles to see which works best for the longest throw.
7. Find a couple of friends, and stage a stick-javelin competition.

Hammer Throw

How to play
An athletic sport in which athletes swing a heavy iron ball on the end of a long steel wire, and attempt to launch it as far as possible into a cone-shaped outdoor target area.

Players
One – hammer throwers compete individually, taking turns to make throws.

Equipment
Hammer – in the men's event, a heavy iron ball about 12cm in diameter, attached to a 1.2m steel wire with a handle. The whole thing weighs around 7kg.

In the women's event, athletes use a smaller (11cm), lighter (4kg) hammer.

Target – a cone-shaped grass (or synthetic grass) pitch similar to that used in discus, but covering a slightly wider 40° area. As in discus, a C-shaped safety cage surrounds the throwing circle on three sides.

Rules
Athletes take turns to throw, to a maximum of three attempts. Stepping over the step-like 'stop box' at the front of the throwing circle results in a foul (disqualified) throw. After three throws the athlete with the longest qualifying throw wins the game.

Decathlon, Heptathlon and Modern Pentathlon

How to play Decathlon
A multi-event athletic competition in which athletes compete in *ten* different track and field events over two days, adding the scores from each in order to decide the overall winner. Olympic decathlon events include almost every type of athletic track and field event, including **high jump**, **long jump**, **shot put**, **javelin**, **discus**, **pole vault**, two types of **sprint**, **hurdles** and a **middle-distance race**.

How to play Heptathlon
A multi-event athletic competition in which female athletes compete in *seven* different track and field events. Basically, it's a decathlon *without* the **discus**, **pole vault** or **100m-sprint** events. Again, scores from each event are totalled in order to decide the overall winner.

How to play Modern Pentathlon
A multi-sport competition in which male or female athletes compete in *five* different events – most quite different from those seen in decathlon and heptathlon. The Olympic modern pentathlon features a 200m **swim**, **horse jumping**, a 3km **cross-country run**, **pistol shooting** and **fencing**!

The rules of the Modern Penthalon state that the winner is the athlete with the most points at the end of all five events.

Players
Multi-event athletes compete individually, taking turns or facing opponents head-to-head in each event.

Equipment
Multi-event athletes use the same equipment – shoes, javelins, poles, trunks, swords, pistols and so on – as the competitors in the individual track and field events.

Give it a go!

Exercise: stage your own heptathlon
Type: skill
Goal: skill, coordination

1. Find a wide, open space with plenty of room to run, jump and throw (and no one to injure).
2. Grab two or more friends, three heavy beanbags, three long bamboo sticks, three frisbees, a long spool of ribbon, some masking tape and a pad and pencil.
3. (Optional) Make three medals: one bronze, one silver and one gold, using a 2p piece, a 50p piece, and a £1 coin. Clip a small bulldog clip on to each one, then thread a piece of ribbon through and tie the ends to make a wide loop, big enough to go over your head.
4. Write the list of events in a column down the left-hand side of the notepad page, then write the competitors' names in a row across the top. This is your scoring grid. The events are: **sprint**, **long jump**, **triple jump**, **shot put**, **javelin**, **discus** and **marathon**.
5. Start with event **number one** – the **sprint**. Choose a starting point and mark out a line using two beanbags and a length of ribbon on the ground. Now mark out a finish line about 100m away. (If you can find two trees within four metres of each other, tape the ribbon at chest height between them, then work backwards from there to mark out a starting line.) Line the

players up, then, all together, say 'Ready, set, GO' and make a dash for the finish. Note the winner on the notepad.

6. Now move on to event **number two** – the **standing long jump**. Go back to your sprint starting line, stand behind it, then one at a time leap as far as you can, landing feet-first. Have one of the other players watch and mark the spot where you landed with a beanbag. Leave it there while the next player jumps, marking his/her jump with the second beanbag. Then repeat for the remaining player(s). Each player gets three attempts. If you jump further than your previous beanbag marker, you can shift it forward to indicate your new record. At the end of all the jumps, the player with the beanbag furthest from the start line wins. Note the winner.

7. Now pick up the beanbags and move back to the starting line for event **number three** – the **triple jump**. This is almost the same as the standing jump, except that you (a) get to take a run-up, (b) have to hop or skip twice before reaching the starting (take-off) line and (c) have to take off from one foot instead of two. Mark your jump with a beanbag as before. Everyone gets three attempts each. At the end, note the winner.

8. Event **number four** is the **standing beanbag shot put**. For this, each player crouches behind the starting line with a beanbag held in one hand, just beneath one ear. To throw, stand, twist your body and launch the beanbag as far as you can, pushing upward and outward with your palm (no overarm throws). Leave the beanbag where it lands while the other players

throw theirs. At the end of the round, mark the beanbag landing spots with a short strip of masking tape (you can write the players' initials on it with the pencil), then proceed to round two. As with the jumps, each player gets three attempts. The longest throw after three rounds wins. Note the winner.

9. Event **number five** is the **bamboo javelin**. Use the starting line as your take-off point, then follow the instructions on page 57 to play the event. Again, you can mark the landing points with masking tape between rounds. The longest throw wins. Note the winner.

10. Event **number six** is the **frisbee discus**. Like javelin, except now you're throwing a frisbee. And to make it harder you also have to release the frisbee from the back (little-finger side) of your hand as you throw it. (Spinning wind-up optional!) Mark the landing spot with tape. The longest throw after three rounds wins. Note the winner.

11. The final event, **number seven**, is the **mini-marathon** or **distance race**. Use Google Maps to create a long-distance course, with a starting point and end point at least two miles apart. Between your school and your house, perhaps. Or maybe just four times around the village. Make sure the route is safe, and that you can stay on grass or pavement (and off the roads) throughout. Once the course is set, everybody sets off together at the starting line, and races to the agreed finish line. To make it interesting, the winner of the mini-marathon gets two 'wins', rather than just one.

12. Now total up the wins on the notepad and declare the victor, based on who won the most. Stage the awards ceremony, complete with medals, and jog a victory lap around the house wearing your medals. Start planning your next heptathlon event right away. Same time next week?

2. Going the Distance

Why can some people run marathons, but others start wheezing after a mile?

*Because distance running not only requires strength, it also requires **fitness** and **endurance**. Some people are born 'fitter' than others, as fitness partly depends on how big your lungs and heart are, and how efficiently they work. But endurance is also a skill – you get better at it with practice. So with the right kind of exercise and training almost anyone can make themselves fitter and build amazing levels of endurance.*

So what's the difference between being fit and being healthy?

The two are related, but not quite the same. **Health** is simply the *absence of disease*, so being healthy means not being sick. **Fitness**, on the other hand, is a slightly bigger idea. Being fit means *being healthy and able to perform physical tasks*.

Can you be healthy without being fit?

Well, you can be *reasonably* healthy without necessarily being *very* fit. But keeping fit, along with healthy eating (or **nutrition**), is very important for staying healthy, especially as you get older. And fitness is *extremely* important to athletes. In short, you can't play many sports well without being fit.

The good news is that no matter how fit (or unfit) you are right now, with the right kind of training, you can get much fitter with *practice*, as fitness (like balance, timing and most other sporting qualities) is a *skill*.

Eating Yourself Healthy Nutrition, or healthy eating, is an essential part of training for most top-level athletes. Swimmers and distance runners, in particular, use up a lot of energy in their daily training, so they have to eat thousands of calories per day just to keep their muscles fuelled. But if you want to reach peak fitness, you can't just scarf down platefuls of burgers, chips and ice cream. For this reason, most athletes avoid eating too many fatty and sugary foods. Instead, they eat a carefully balanced diet, with plenty of **protein** to build and repair muscle, vegetables for **essential vitamins** and **fibre**, and **complex carbohydrates** to build slow-release energy stores. That means a daily diet of eggs, milk, fish, lean meats, beans, salad greens, potatoes, brown rice, pasta and wholewheat bread.

Fitness is a *skill*? I've heard of 'getting fit' and 'keeping fit'. Are you telling me you can get 'extra fit' too?

Yep, that's *exactly* what I'm telling you. Not everyone can become as fit as an Olympic cyclist or swimmer. If you're born with a heart or lung problem, there may be some limits to how fit you can get. On the flipside, some athletes are simply born with amazingly efficient hearts, lungs and muscles.

But most healthy people can easily *double* (or even *triple*) their fitness and endurance levels with the right kind of training.

What have hearts and lungs got to do with being fit?

How well your heart and lungs work has *everything* to do with being fit. Fitness and endurance are all about how well – and how quickly – you can get oxygen to your muscles. And in the human body that's the job of the heart, the lungs and the rest of the **cardiovascular system**.

Wait, the *what?*

In the last chapter, remember, we learned that organs in the body are arranged into **organ systems** – each one with a special role in the body. Then we looked at one of these systems, the **musculoskeletal system**, and found out why it's so important to sporting movements (or, for that matter, *any* type of movement).

So now we're going to add *another* organ system, and see how it all fits in.

Your **cardiovascular system** (or **CV system**, for short) includes your heart, lungs, arteries, veins and other blood vessels. Its main job is to **deliver oxygen** – dissolved into the bloodstream from the **lungs** – to hungry muscles, tissues and organs all over your body. The oxygen is carried in the bloodstream by **red blood cells**, bound to special oxygen-trapping proteins called **haemoglobins.**

The bloodstream also carries **nutrients**. These are extracted from the food in your stomach and intestines, and dissolve into the bloodstream as **sugars**, **fatty acids**, **amino acids** and **salts**. This is important, as muscles and other tissues use these nutrients to create **energy stores**. Without a constant supply of **oxygen** *and* **energy**, your muscles stop working pretty quickly. Oh, and you'd die.

Just as importantly, your cardiovascular system also *stops toxic wastes from building up* in your tissues, by delivering them to the lungs and kidneys for removal. These toxic nasties include **carbon dioxide** (the stuff you breathe out with every breath) and **lactic acid**, which we'll be finding out a bit more about later on.

OK, I get that. But I still don't see what that has to do with being fit.

Being **fit** (biologically speaking) means having a **well-developed cardiovascular system** which is very good at supplying nutrients and oxygen to the muscles.

During hard exercise, the muscles use up the body's energy and oxygen stores very quickly.

Fit people have no trouble replacing these stores, because their CV systems are good at getting oxygen (especially) from the lungs to the muscles. So their muscles keep working for longer, and they can keep running, rowing or swimming for a long time.

Unfit people simply *can't replace* the used-up oxygen and energy *quickly enough*. Their hearts, lungs and blood vessels can't take in enough oxygen, can't get enough oxygen into the blood and can't shift the blood around the body quickly enough to supply the hungry muscles.

Starved of energy and oxygen, the muscles begin to shut down, and **fatigue** sets in.

This is why unfit people pant for breath, then collapse in a heap, while fit people around them run on. They're *trying* to get more oxygen into their bodies, but they *can't*, so their leg muscles give out. Or, more often, their brains tell them to lie down *before* they collapse.

So why doesn't this happen when you're sprinting? I mean, more or less everyone can run a *short* distance without collapsing, right?

That's because it takes *time* for the oxygen and energy to run out. Most of your muscles have their own little energy stores, which are built up while you're resting. They're just sitting there waiting to be used. Similarly (unless you've been holding your breath for the last ten minutes) you *start* a sprint with oxygen *already* in your bloodstream.

When you start sprinting, your leg muscles pump away furiously, using up energy and oxygen as they do so. But, for most people, unless you *continue* sprinting for more than thirty seconds, you've still got plenty of energy and oxygen stores left by the time you stop running.

This is why more or less everyone can sprint a short distance without collapsing. With or without training, the sprint is pretty much over before fitness comes into play. But run a bit further, say 400m rather than 100m, and the difference between fit and unfit people becomes very clear.

So the further you run the fitter you need to be?

Exactly. That's why fitness is *extremely* important for

runners, cyclists and other endurance athletes, as, in general, the longer the duration of exercise, the greater the role the CV system plays in performance.

It's *less* important to sprinters, as a 100m sprint has little or no cardiovascular involvement – it's more to do with explosive strength, and the race is over before fitness and endurance really come into play.

Likewise, jumps and throws just require one quick, explosive burst of strength from the arms, legs and core muscles. But, since high jumpers and shot putters aren't asked to do this over and over again, fitness and endurance don't matter so much.

But marathons and 1,000m swimming races require tip-top fitness levels. So a great deal of training is needed to improve the functions of your heart, lungs and other cardiovascular organs.

So what's the best way to *get* fit, if you're not already?

We'll be looking at fitness training, and how it works, in more detail throughout this chapter. In general, how you train for fitness depends on which sport you're interested in doing.

Distance running is the most common way to build endurance, but it's not the only way. Runners run, swimmers swim, rowers row. Done long enough, even **walking** will help build endurance over time. Many endurance athletes use a *combination* of these to increase their fitness and endurance levels. For example, running in the mornings, and swimming or rowing in the afternoons.

That sounds like pretty hard work.

It is. Elite athletes take their fitness training very seriously, and may run, swim or row for several hours a day, just to stay in peak condition.

What if you're *not* a champion athlete? How fit do you need to be, and how much should you run or swim?

For young people under the age of eighteen just looking to stay fit and healthy, most doctors and sports scientists say that an hour of moderate exercise every day should be enough.

But if you want to do a bit more no one's going to stop you!

Smoking – the Fitness Killer For decades now, we've known that smoking cigarettes leads to damage and diseases of the lungs. So it should be obvious that if you want to get (or stay) fit then smoking is a pretty stupid idea. The toxic carbon monoxide found in cigarette smoke binds to the haemoglobin proteins in your blood cells more powerfully than oxygen.

So smoking decreases the amount of oxygen you can hold in your bloodstream, and how much of it can be passed rapidly to your needy muscles. At the very least, smoking will decrease your endurance levels by 10% or more. At worst, it could cause blood clots that lead to lung disease, heart disease or strokes. For this reason, most serious athletes do not smoke. It makes about as much sense as running a race wearing iron shoes and a snorkel.

Distance Running, Walking and Cycling

How far can you run before your legs fall off?

*Nobody knows for sure, but, provided they train for it and feed themselves well, it seems that there's no limit to how far an elite athlete can run. Ultramarathon runner **Dean Karnazes** can run 350 miles (480km) without stopping, and once ran fifty marathons in fifty days.*

Seriously? *350 miles*, non-stop?

Yep. That's the same as running about *thirteen 26-mile marathons*.

Like finishing the London Marathon, then doing it *twelve more times*?

Exactly. And that's *without stopping* to rest or sleep. *With sleep*, elite distance runners like Dean Karnazes seem *unstoppable*.

In 2006, he ran fifty marathons in fifty days – one in each of America's fifty states. Stopping only for four to five hours of sleep per night, he racked up a total distance of over **1,300 miles** (2,000km).

After completing his final run, the New York City Marathon, he then decided to *run home*.

To San Francisco. Over *3,000 miles* (4,800km) away.

What?! Is he mental?

Nope. Just really, really good at running. In 2011, he ran another 3,000 miles from Disneyland (California) to New York, clocking 40–50 miles (64–80km) per day for eighty-five days straight.

But that seems *impossible*. I mean, how could he *do that* without his heart *exploding* or something?
Well, it seems that Mr Karnazes was *born* a little special. Scientific tests have revealed that he has incredible **muscular endurance**, meaning that his muscles can work for an *extraordinarily* long time before getting tired. (We'll learn more about this later on in the chapter.) Because of this, his heart doesn't have to work so hard to resupply his muscles with oxygen, and it's never in any danger of failing or exploding.

'Run when you can, walk if you have to, crawl if you must; just never give up.'

Dean Karnazes,
ultramarathon runner

That said, *thousands* of otherwise average people are now running ultramarathon races too. The human race, it seems, was *born* for long-distance running.

Born for it? What d'you mean?
Well, long before we got busy farming, building cities and staging international sporting competitions, human beings survived for thousands of years on their wits and hunting

Distance Running

How to play

An endurance sport played on roads, outdoor trails or large, indoor arenas. Athletes race each other on foot, pacing themselves so that they can cover the distance quickly without wearing out. Where sprints are battles of speed and power, distance races are battles of technique, timing, endurance and willpower. Middle distance races include the **800m**, the **1,500m** and the **3,000m steeplechase**. Long-distance events include the **10,000m**, the 26-mile (42km) **marathon**, and even 50–3,000 mile (80–5,000km) **ultramarathons**.

Players

One – runners generally compete individually, running against competitors or against the clock.

Equipment

Shoes – distance runners use a wide range of shoe types. Some run in thin-soled, split-toed 'minimal' shoes, or even run barefoot, but most runners use leather or plastic running shoes with cushioned heels, with or without metal spikes in the soles for grip.

Backpack, water bottle – used by ultramarathoners to store food and water for their incredibly long runs, which can take several *days* (or even *weeks*) to complete.

ability. Catching forest and woodland animals like rabbits and wild boar was simple enough. You just sneaked up on them with a spear or bow and arrow. But hunting wary, fleet-footed herding animals like antelope – across wide, flat plains and grasslands – was much harder.

On an open plain, we couldn't hope to sneak up on a herd of antelope. And we could never hope to run *faster* than an antelope (which, after all, can hit over 60mph as they run from cheetahs and lionesses). So we came up with a different tactic. Instead of *sprinting* after our prey, we began *jogging* after them instead.

Jogging?!

Yep. Jogging. As we already learned in chapter one, antelope (and plenty of other animals) can easily outrun humans over a short distance. But here's the thing: very few animals can **cool themselves** by **sweating** the way humans can. After a brief sprint, lionesses, cheetahs and antelopes alike have to sit down, rest and cool off. Our human ancestors took advantage of this, jogging after frightened antelope, catching up with them and never allowing them to rest for long between sprints. After a while, the prey would be unable to run any further, so the hunter could just walk up to it, and spear it or simply bash it with a rock.

This is called **endurance hunting** or a **running hunt**, and it seems that the human hunters who were good at it tended to survive better than those who weren't. Over time, then, the distance runners survived and had babies, and the whole human race evolved to be better and better at running distances. As Dean Karnazes proves, we've yet to discover the absolute limit to how far we can run. But it now seems clear that, with the proper training, more or less *anyone* can work up to running 30, 50, 100 miles or more.

But *how*? What sort of training would you have to do?

For the most part, **cardiovascular** (or simply **cardio**) training.

As I said earlier on, endurance is a *trainable skill*. You train it by improving three things: **cardiovascular fitness**, **muscular endurance** and **efficiency of movement**. We'll look at the last two in a little while. For now, let's just look at cardio fitness, and how it's affected by **cardio training**.

Done correctly, cardio training makes the cardiovascular system *more efficient* at **pumping blood** and **delivering oxygen** to the skeletal muscles.

Basically, with cardio training, you're trying to do two things:

1. Increase your body's *maximum rate of oxygen uptake.*
2. Increase the *amount of work your muscles can do* before tiredness (or **fatigue**) begins to set in.

But how can it change how much oxygen you take in? Does it make your lungs bigger or something?

Not really. For starters, there's not a great deal of space inside your chest into which your lungs could expand. Your ribs press against them from the sides, and your stomach, intestines and other organs press up on them from below.* So, even if you *could* make them larger, you'd have trouble inflating them to their full size.

---

* Well, technically they lie against the diaphragm, which is the sheet of muscle that separates the lungs from the organs of the abdomen. But since the diaphragm partly controls how much the lungs can expand the effect is the same.

Provided that your lungs are working well and you're breathing correctly, your **rate of oxygen uptake** depends not on your lungs, but on something else.

What's that?

Your **heart**. Your heart doesn't take oxygen from the air, but it *is* responsible for getting the oxygen from the lungs to the muscles. And the harder you work the more important this blood-and-oxygen pump becomes.

Race Walking

How to play
An endurance sport – also known as **power walking** or **speed walking** – in which athletes speed walk their way through a long-distance road race. One foot must stay in contact with the ground at all times, and any athlete who skips into a run is warned, then disqualified. In many ways, speed walking is much harder than running, as the shorter, less efficient movements used are much harder work.

Players
One – speed walkers compete individually, racing against other athletes.

Equipment
Shoes – speed walkers wear thin-soled leather or plastic running shoes, which allow the feet to contact the ground more fully.

When you're at rest (i.e. not doing much of anything), your muscles don't need much oxygen or bloodflow. So only 15–20% of your blood goes to the muscles. The rest goes to your brain, digestive organs and other bits of the body.

But during hard exercise like running or swimming your muscles start burning through stored energy and oxygen very quickly. So the amount of blood flowing to your muscles *has to increase* to 80–85%, just to keep your muscles supplied with oxygen.

So how does it get there? Well, first, the **blood vessels** (**arteries**, **veins**, **arterioles** and **venules**) that feed and drain your working muscles *open up*. Meanwhile, the vessels that feed the brain and digestive system *close up* a bit. This *redirects blood flow* towards the muscles. It's a bit like damming a river to redirect water into a new reservoir.

But if all this redirected blood and oxygen is going to get to the muscles *in time* then the heart will also have to *pump harder and faster*. And this is exactly what happens.

Is that why your heartbeat feels stronger, and your pulse goes faster, when you run?

Yep – spot on. During a hard run, ride or swim, your **heart rate** (**HR**) *can double or triple*, from a typical resting rate of 60–90bpm (beats per minute) to around 200bpm.

The amount of blood pumped with each stroke of the heart pump – known as the **stroke volume** (**SV**) – also increases as you work. It goes from a volume of 50–80 millilitres per beat when you're just sitting about, to around 110–130 millilitres per beat during hard exercise.

Together, these two things (**HR** and **SV**) create your **cardiac output** (**CO**). In short, you just multiply one by the other to get the *total volume of blood shifted by the heart every minute*. So:

HR x SV = CO

On average, your total **cardiac output** rises from about *5l/min (litres per minute)* at rest to *30–40l/min* during exercise.

In other words, at rest, the amount of blood your heart shifts per minute would *fill five tall milk cartons*. During exercise, your heart shifts enough blood in one minute to fill the *fuel tank of a small car*.

So does a marathon runner's heart beat really fast, then? So it can shift more blood per minute?

You might think so, because if the heart rate (HR) goes up, then we can see from the sums above that the cardiac output (CO) would automatically go up too, right?

Right. Makes sense.

Unfortunately, that can't really happen. At around 200 beats per minute, the heart is under a great deal of strain, and it *can't beat much faster* without wearing out the cardiac muscle, which would eventually lead to a heart attack, or **cardiac arrest**.

And, in fact, trained athletes' hearts beat *slower* than those of less-fit people for a given rate of exercise.

This is because training doesn't make their hearts beat *faster* – it makes them beat *more efficiently*. The heart is basically made of cardiac muscle tissue, fed by a system of blood vessels on the outside, and woven through with nerves that help regulate the heartbeat. Just as strength training increases the size of skeletal muscles, over time,

Track Cycling

How to play
An endurance sport played on outdoor roads and tracks, or large indoor circuits called **velodromes**. In **road races**, athletes on racing cycles compete head-to-head or against the clock – pacing themselves to cover hilly, long-distance courses rapidly while avoiding complete exhaustion. In velodrome events, riders race round a banked, oval track, trying to beat the clock, or beat each other to the finish line.

Players
In most road races and velodrome events, riders compete as individuals, racing each other or the clock to win. But there are also team and relay cycling events in which teams of two to four riders work together to beat rival teams.

Equipment
Racing cycle – these differ widely depending on the type of event. Most racing bikes have lightweight aluminium or carbon-fibre frames and curved 'drop' handlebars that allow the rider to keep their head and body low (avoiding air resistance) while steering. Some also have solid **disc wheels**, rather than traditional **spoked wheels**. These create smoother air flow (and less drag) around the wheels.
Cycle helmet – a lightweight foam-and-plastic helmet that protects the skull in the event of a high-speed crash. Some also have a tapering shape, like an aircraft's nose or tail, which helps decrease air resistance and drag around the head. Anything for a little more speed!

cardio training, like long-distance running and swimming, actually increases the amount of cardiac muscle tissue, and the *size of an athlete's heart*. This, in turn, increases their **stroke volume** (**SV**) and the overall **cardiac output** (**CO**). This lessens the need for a higher pulse rate.

As a result, elite endurance athletes have lower resting pulse rates (around 40–60, rather than 70–80), and can run, swim or cycle for *longer* before their pulse rates gradually rise to their maximum.

Big-hearted Pedallers American cyclist **Lance Armstrong** won the gruelling Tour de France long-distance race a record seven times in a row. Tests have shown that his heart is 30% larger than that of the average person, and his resting heart rate is just 32–34bpm. Spanish cycling champion **Miguel Indurain**, who won the Tour de France five times between 1991 and 1996, had an *even larger* heart, and a resting pulse rate of just 28bpm. At one beat every two seconds, these guys' hearts were barely even ticking over!

So the *fitter* you are, the *more efficiently* your heart is working, and the *slower your HR* is for a given pace or intensity of exercise. This is true whether you're **running**, **swimming**, **speed walking**, **cycling** or **cross-country skiing**. *All* endurance events like this require peak levels of fitness, and you can't be a champion in any of them without this kind of training.

Sigh. Better get moving, then, I s'pose. I've got some serious fit-i-fication to do . . .

Here's the good news, though: doing cardio training for any one of these sports will also make you better at the others. So training for **distance running** will make you better at **distance swimming**, training for **swimming** will make you better at **distance skiing**, and so on. Once you're fit for one sport, you're fit for them all!

If you want to test and improve your cardiovascular fitness, try the exercises on pages 83–5.

❛Pain is temporary. Quitting lasts forever.❜

Lance Armstrong,
champion road-racing cyclist,
and seven-times winner of the Tour de France

In general, the *fitter* you are, the *lower* your resting pulse rate will be. The average adult has a resting pulse rate of 60–100bpm. For children it can be a little higher, at 70–120bpm.

Elite endurance athletes – including champion runners, cyclists and cross-country skiers – can have resting pulse rates of 40bpm or less.

Also, the fitter you are the longer it will take for your pulse rate to rise to its maximum level. The maximum, in bpm, is usually **220 minus your age.** So if you're ten years old, it'll be around 210bpm, but if you're forty years old it'll be around 180bpm.

In any case, after two minutes of hard exercise, unfit

Give it a go!

Exercise: fitness test
Type: cardiovascular
Goal: measuring your personal fitness level

1. Grab a stopwatch, or watch with a second hand.
2. Press two fingers into *one* side (not both!) of your neck, just below your jawline. Don't press too hard – just go deep enough to feel your pulse beating away in the arteries of your neck.
3. Count how many times your pulse beats in the next thirty seconds. To do this, count the **beats**, but watch the **clock**.
4. Now multiply this by two to find your **resting pulse rate**. (So if you counted 35 beats, multiply by two to get a resting pulse rate of 70.)
5. Immediately drop the watch and *exercise for the next two minutes* straight. You can **run on the spot** (lifting your knees as high as possible) do **press-ups**, do **jump-squats** (see previous chapter) – any one of these will do. Just don't stop. Keep going, as fast as you can, for two minutes.
6. Now **immediately** repeat steps 1–4. This will give you a number for your pulse rate during exercise.

people will find themselves close to their maximum heart rate, while fit people will be less than halfway between their resting and maximum rates.

Give it a go!

Exercise: gear-change breathing
Type: cardiovascular
Goal: improving your fitness and endurance

1. Put on some suitable clothes, and go for a walk outside.
2. As you walk, try *breathing in* on one footstep, and *out* on the next. (Like a soldier's march – in-out, in-out, in-out . . .) Continue this for one minute.
3. Now *stretch the inhales and exhales* so that they take *two* footsteps to complete. So now you go in-in, out-out, in-in, out-out. Don't do this in two sips or blasts – just make the inhale or exhale longer, so that they end after precisely two footsteps. Again, keep going for at least one minute.
4. Now try three footsteps in, three footsteps out. Continue for another minute.
5. Now try four in, four out, for one minute more.
6. Now come back down to three in, three out, for thirty seconds.
7. Now down to two in, two out for the next thirty seconds.
8. Now back down to one in, one out for thirty more seconds.
9. Now continue walking, with whatever breath pattern you find the most comfortable. It might be two in, two out, three in three out – it's up to you.
10. Congratulations – you've just learned to match your breathing to your exercise.

The next day, try the whole thing again, but jog, rather than walk. You'll soon find that your endurance and fitness increase, as relaxed breathing will help you walk or run further without stopping. Before you know it, you could be running marathons and swimming for miles!

Swimming

Why don't swimming champions swim like sharks?

*Because human swimmers – even Olympic champions – aren't built like fish, so trying to swim like a shark wouldn't make them go any faster. Instead, champion swimmers focus on being **like** sharks:* sleek, streamlined *and* efficient in the water.

Wait . . . so they're not *built* like sharks, and can't *swim* like sharks . . . but they still try to *be* like sharks?
Exactly.

I'm confused.
OK, look at it this way: what makes sharks such speedy swimmers?

Err, their long tails?

That's part of it, yes. Fast-swimming sharks like the **mako shark** can hit very high speeds underwater by whipping their **tails** and **caudal fins** (tail fins) from side to side, quickly and powerfully. But not only do human swimmers *not have tail fins*, they also lack the *muscles* to make these powerful movements.

Hang on, swimmers *do* have muscles. Pretty big ones too, if they're Olympic athletes.

Right. But their most powerful muscles don't run down the sides of their bodies, as they do in a shark. In fact, the muscles on the outsides of our legs, and either side of our spine and ribcage, are relatively weak in humans.

Because we evolved to *walk* and *run*, rather than *swim*, our strongest muscles lie in front of and behind our spines (including the **erector spinae**, **trapezius** and **abdominal muscles**), and in front of and behind our legs (the **hamstrings**, **quadriceps** and **gluteus maximus muscles**). Hence, our bodies are good at bending forward and backwards (or curling and straightening), but they're pretty rubbish at wiggling from side to side, like a shark.

Aha! But don't *dolphins* swim by wiggling their bodies up and down too? Couldn't we learn to move like them?

Well, in some ways, champion swimmers (especially those who do the butterfly stroke) do just this – waving their bodies up and down to gain more power and speed in the water. But human swimmers still lack the huge, flat tail that transfers a dolphin's vertical wiggles into a powerful swimming stroke. So, for the most part, a swimmer's power comes from his or her arms. Leg kicks *add* speed, certainly. But without wearing fins on our feet (as scuba divers do, but swimmers do not) kicking *alone* wouldn't get you anywhere fast. So, whether you're doing a crawl, backstroke, breast-stroke or butterfly, it's your *arms* that are really driving you through the water.

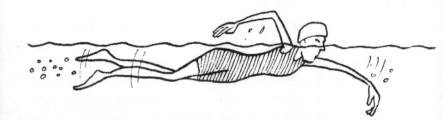

Swimming

How to play

An endurance water sport with many different events held at large indoor or outdoor pools, in which athletes race through the water in lanes marked by ropes or buoys. The aim is to beat other competitors to the finish over a fixed distance or set number of laps. A range of swimming techniques or strokes are used, including **backstroke**, **breast-stroke**, **butterfly** and **freestyle**. Some events allow only one type of stroke, while others allow swimmers to alternate stroke types across different legs of the race. Events include 50m, 100m and 200m **sprints**, 4 x 100m and 4 x 200m **relays**, 400m and 1,500m **distance races** and 10km (6.2-mile) **marathons**.

Players

One to four. Swimmers mostly compete individually, racing against other solo swimmers. But in relay races, teams of four swimmers take turns to complete equal parts of the 400–800m race distance.

Equipment

Pool – Olympic swimming pools are 50m long and 25m wide, with long floating ropes that divide them into eight lanes of equal width. Unlike most recreational pools, they don't have a 'deep end' – the depth (1.8m) is the same throughout.

Goggles – these allow swimmers to see underwater, so that they can keep their heads down and reduce drag while also orientating themselves by looking at the bottom of the pool.

Swim cap – rubber or latex cap worn by most swimmers to decrease the drag and resistance caused by free-flowing hair.

Bodysuit – worn by many swimmers to decrease drag and help them cut through the water more smoothly.

So how *do* champion swimmers make themselves faster than everyone else?

They train hard to increase their cardiovascular fitness (as we saw in the last section), and also to perfect their swimming **form** (or **shape**) and the **efficiency** of their movements in the water.

How does changing their shape make a difference?

Well, in many ways, a swimmer trying to cut through the water is like an aircraft trying to cut through the air. Of course, swimmers **float**, which makes it easier for them to stay 'up' compared with a jet aeroplane. So falling (or sinking) due to gravity is less of a problem. But, just like a jet aeroplane, a swimmer's body is *slowed down* by **drag**.

As an aeroplane's engines push it forward through the air, the air rushes past the nose of the aircraft and flows over its wings and body. Friction between the air and these surfaces slows the aircraft down. This is called drag. To counter this, aeroplane designers make them **streamlined** or **aerodynamic**. They avoid having things (other than the wings, which are kind of important!) sticking out from the sides of the plane's body, and try to make it *one sleek, smooth-sided shape*, so that air flows easily by, and drag is reduced.

What has that got to do with swimmers and sharks?

Good question. Sharks and swimmers are affected by drag too. As they try to power through the water, friction from the water around them drags on their bodies and slows them down. In fact, since water is much *thicker* (or *more dense*) than air, the effects of drag are even *stronger* in the water.

Sharks have managed to get round this by evolving a streamlined body shape. They're shaped like swimming missiles. Their bodies are long, thin tubes with a cone-shaped nose at the front (which parts the water before the shark as it goes) and short, flat fins along the side and top which allow the smooth movement of water around them.

Shark Suits From the 1990s onwards, some champion swimmers, including Olympic gold medallists Michael Phelps and Ian 'Thorpedo' Thorpe, began wearing full-length bodysuits to reduce the effect of drag in the water. These suits feature tiny plastic ridges (or 'riblets'), which mimic the interlocking scales of a shark skin. The riblets help to break up pockets of turbulent (or churning) water that cause extra drag, and aid the flow of water around the swimmer. Physicists say these suits make little or no difference to the total drag experienced by a swimmer, anyway. But officials were worried enough by the full-length 'fast suits' that they banned them in Olympic competitions from 2010 onwards. Now male competitors' suits cannot extend above the waist or below the knee, while female competitors' suits can go from the shoulders to the knees.

Now compare this with a human swimmer. We have rounded heads and flat faces, which drag in the water every time we raise them to breathe. We have flailing arms and legs, which *drag* in the water as we try to use them to push *through* it. We *can* swim, but we're not *built* to do it the way a shark is.

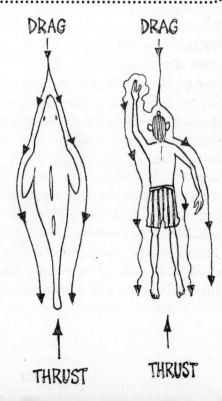

DRAG

DRAG

THRUST

THRUST

So what's the answer?

The answer is to try to make the shape of your swimming stroke as streamlined and shark-like as possible. And that's exactly what champion swimmers do. True, they spend many hours building their muscles, so that they can push and pull themselves through the water with more force. But they spend even *more* time practising their strokes in the pool, trying to make themselves glide through the water with less drag.

This means making sure that fingers and toes stay together, hands pierce the water fingertip first, and elbows, knees and other body parts don't stick out and drag in the water as they swim. Anything that sticks out will slow them down, making their movements less *powerful* and *efficient*. Swimmers practise for hours – often wearing snorkels, so that they don't have to worry about lifting their heads to breathe – to create the perfect, shark-like, gliding stroke.

I've got a snorkel. But they won't let me wear it at the pool.

Next time, just tell them you're in training for the Olympics, and you're working on your swimming stroke. Maybe they'll let you.

Good idea! So are swimmers the only ones who practise their movements like that?

Not at all. The final piece of the endurance-training puzzle, for **swimmers**, **skiers** and all kinds of **endurance athletes**, is *perfecting their movement*.

After all, two competing athletes may have the same level of *fitness* and *endurance*, but if one of them has *poor form*, or an *inefficient* way of moving, then he will be working harder just to keep the same pace.

Really?
Yep. If you don't believe me, try this:

1. Do five press-ups on the floor, as quickly as you can.
2. Now get into the press-up position and get ready to do five more. But, before you start, tense every muscle in your body – your arms, legs, stomach, back, face, everything. Now keep it all tense while you do your five press-ups.
3. Finally, do five more, this time focusing on staying as relaxed as possible throughout.

You probably found that the middle set of five press-ups (when you were tense) seemed much more difficult, right?

[Gasp, pant!] . . . Right . . .
That's because you were tensing and involving *more muscles than you needed* to do the press-up, so your movements were *not efficient*. The third time, you were probably only using the muscles you needed to lift you up. So your movements were more efficient, and it all felt easier.

The same thing applies to swimming strokes. If you tense too many muscles, or try to push or pull at the water too hard, then you're using more muscles than you need, your shape in the water changes and the whole thing becomes harder than it needs to be. If you want to learn how to swim effortlessly, like a champion swimmer, then try the exercise at the end of this section.

So to be champion runner or swimmer, being fit's not enough?

Right. To be truly great at running, swimming or cycling, you also have to perfect your relaxed movement, so that you can leave the muscles to do as little work as possible (leaving plenty of energy in reserve for that sprint finish!).

This requires a keen sense of balance, timing and relaxation. Which can only come with **expert coaching**, **lots of practice** and **muscle memory**.

For now, how would you like to be able to swim without effort, like a shark or dolphin does?

Of course I would!
In that case, try this . . .

Give it a go!

Exercise: relaxed swimming
Type: skill
Goal: improving your swimming movements

1. Go to a local pool when there aren't too many people about. Try to find a clear lane in which to practise. Make sure you're at a depth where you can stand up comfortably on the bottom. Wear goggles.
2. Swim one length of the pool as you normally would, front crawl (freestyle). Feel how hard you have to work to complete the length.
3. Now try this: instead of swimming, put your arms by your sides, push your feet off the bottom and glide forward as far as you can. Keep your arms by your sides, your face pointed down and the back of your head in a straight line with your spine. Try to relax and float in the water as

you go. Go across the whole pool this way in a series of gliding leaps. Don't kick with your legs – just glide.
4. Try to feel how keeping your spine and head straight – and your arms tight to your body – streamlines you like a shark, allowing you to cut through the water more smoothly and quickly.
5. Now repeat, but this time extend one hand in front of you (like Superman!), keeping your arm straight and tilted down at 45° towards the bottom. *Alternate hands* at the start of each push-and-glide (i.e. every time you push off the bottom). Do one more length like this.
6. Now try swimming a length, still keeping your spine straight and face down (until you need to breathe, of course!). As you crawl with your arms, make sure your flattened hands return to the same position, 45° in front of you and down, every time. Keep your kicking very light. Don't thrash your feet like a motorboat engine – just give little kicks to tilt your body from side to side, and let your arms and streamlined body do the work.

Practise all this, and you should soon feel your swimming stroke getting easier and faster – covering more distance with each pull of your arms. Congratulations – now you can swim with shark-like smoothness!

My goal is one Olympic gold medal. Not many people in this world can say, "I'm an Olympic gold medallist."

Michael Phelps,
champion swimmer and winner
of *fourteen* Olympic gold medals

Rowing, Canoeing and Kayaking

Are rowing, canoeing and kayaking all the same thing?

Nope – not at all. They all involve racing a long boat through the water. But rowers, canoeists and kayakers **propel** *their boats in quite different ways. Rowers sit facing* backwards, *while canoeists and kayakers sit facing* forward. *Rowers grip boat-mounted* **oars**, *while canoeists and kayakers wield single or double-ended* **paddles.** *And while rowers* use almost every muscle in their bodies *to pull their boats through the water, for the most part, canoeists and kayakers* use their upper bodies alone.

Rowers sit *backwards*? Wouldn't that make their boats go backwards too?

Well, that depends on how you look at it. A rowing boat travels in the *opposite* direction to the way the pilot (rower, or crew of rowers) is facing, whereas canoes and kayaks travel in the same direction the pilot is facing. Either way, the pilot is **pushing water backwards** to make the boat travel **forward**.

Eh? How does that work?

Simple – as the famous physicist, mathematician and all-round genius **Isaac Newton** first said, in the world of movement and physics, **every action has an equal and opposite reaction**. In rowing and canoeing, it's easy to see this idea in action.

To make the boat go forward, the rower or canoeist places a flattened blade (on the end of a long pole or handle) into the water, and uses it to *push water backwards*. The equal and opposite reaction to this is simple: *the boat* (complete with rower or canoeist) *moves forward*. The harder and faster they drive the water back, the faster the boat will accelerate in the opposite direction.

The main difference between rowing, canoeing and kayaking is *how* that water is pushed backwards. Canoeists and kayakers sit facing the direction of travel, and paddle with *alternating backward pushes* to the left and right side of the boat. They push the water *behind themselves,* and the boat travels forward. Rowers, on the other hand, sit backwards in the boat, pulling on **bevelling oars** that shift the water (as they see it) *in front of themselves,* or towards their feet.

Aren't oars and paddles the same thing?

Not quite. A **rowing oar** is basically a long pole with a flattened blade at one end. In a rowing boat, the oars thread through special pivoting rings attached to the sides of the boat, called **oarlocks** or **rowlocks**.

A rower may sit holding the handles of **two oars** (one in each hand), the paddle ends of which extend out to the sides and dip in and out of the water. This kind of two-oar rowing is called **sculling**.

Alternatively, a rower may hold a *single* oar – gripping the handle with both hands – which extends out to *one side of the boat* only. This is simply called **rowing**.

But if there's only one oar, and it only sticks out to one side, won't that make the rowing boat go round in circles?

Well spotted! Yes, it would. The equal and opposite reaction of pushing the water backwards *on one side of the boat only* would be to drive the **bow** (or nose-end) of the boat forward *and* to the opposite side. Row only on the left, and the bow will veer right. Row only on the right, and the bow will veer left.

That's why single-oar rowers always work in **pairs**, **fours** or **eights**. Provided that there's an *even number of rowers* – and an *equal number of left and right oars* in the water – their left-and-right-side, backward-pushing forces will be *balanced*, and the equal and opposite reaction will *move the bow straight ahead*. This is why you see two-, four- and eight-person rowing crews, but not threes, fives or sevens.

Rowing

How to play

An endurance sport held in outdoor water courses, in which athletes use two oars (one in each hand) to row thin, sleek watercraft. The boats race head-to-head for the win, or against the clock in time-trial events, powered by solo rowers, or teams of up to **eight** working together. Rowers must use their entire bodies to make powerful movements, and rowing teams must have perfect timing in order to build and maintain top speeds. So this is a game of skill and timing, as well as raw strength and stamina.

Players
One to nine.

In **single-scull** events, rowers compete individually, one per boat.

In **pairs** or **double-scull** events, pairs of rowers work together.

In **quad** and **coxless-four events**, teams of four rowers work as one.

In **coxed-four** and **coxed-eight** events, teams of four or eight rowers work together under the direction of an extra crew member, the **coxswain** (or simply **cox**). The cox does not row, but sits facing the crew – steering the boat, coaching the rowers, judging the pace and telling them when to accelerate or sprint.

Equipment

Racing boat – a long, thin, plastic or carbon-fibre shell, with footplates and sliding seats for each sculler. The sliding seat allows the sculler to move back and forth, bending and straightening the knees to provide driving power from the legs. The footplate attaches to the rower's shoes, holding the feet in place* so that they don't slip during the rowing movement. Racing shells vary in length from 8m for single sculls to 20m for coxed eights.

Oars – long wooden or carbon-fibre poles, with a flat blade at one end and two adjustable rubber grips for the hands. These lock into special oar-holders (or **oarlocks**) attached to the boat, which allow the oars to rotate without slipping through and falling into the water. Again, oars vary in length from 3m single-sculling oars to the 4m rowing oars used by larger teams.

---

* Don't worry – rowing shoes have special velcro fasteners so that the rowers can escape if the boat capsizes!

What about canoes and kayaks?

Instead of long oars, each **canoeist** uses a single, stubby **paddle**. The paddle has a shorter shaft (usually 1–1.5m) with a T-shaped horizontal handle at the top. The canoeist grips the handle with one hand and the shaft with the other, holding the paddle *vertically* above the water, to one side of the body (and the boat). He or she then paddles by dipping the blade down into the water and scooping the water backwards in a vertical churning motion.

Wouldn't that one-sided paddling make the boat go in circles too?

Right. So, to get around this, canoeists either work in pairs (like rowers), or paddle *first on the left side, then the right*, using **alternating strokes**. This nudges the bow from side to side a little, but, provided they keep the power and number of strokes on each side the same, the boat will travel (more or less) straight.

Kayakers use very similar boats to canoeists, but their **paddles** and **paddling methods** are different. A kayak paddle is a long pole with a *flat blade at both ends*. Kayakers hold these double-ended paddles in two hands, with one clenched fist on either side of the chest.

From there, the kayaker dips first the left end, then the right end of the paddle into the water, and uses a **rolling, crawling motion** to make alternating strokes to the left and right sides of the kayak. Again, the bow noses to the left and right a little with each push, but if the kayaker keeps their strokes even the kayak will move happily forward.

They all sound like pretty hard work. Which one is hardest?

Well, the answer to that one will depend on whether you ask a rower, a canoeist or a kayaker! But one thing's for certain: rowing uses (and requires) *more muscles* than either canoeing or kayaking. For this reason, many would say rowing is the toughest of the three.

Why does rowing use more muscles?
In short, because a full rowing stroke involves both the *upper* and *lower* body.

For the most part, canoeists and kayakers sit fairly still in their boats, using powerful twisting motions of the arms, shoulders and torso to drive their paddles through the water. Some canoeists kneel rather than sit, but, again, the legs don't move much, so their lower bodies don't take much part in the paddling movement.

Rowing is *completely* different. In a competitive rowing boat, each rower braces their feet against a **footplate** on the floor of the boat, and sits on a **sliding seat**, which rolls back and forth as the rowers bend and straighten their knees. By pushing with the feet and shifting their bodies backwards with each pull of the oars, a rower connects the powerful muscles of the legs to those of the torso and arms, and puts his or her whole **bodyweight** behind each pull.

‘*The pain of rowing is the scream of lungs, legs, back and muscles. That's just one stroke. Multiply that by 240 strokes in a 2,000m race.*’

Steve Redgrave,
legendary British rower and winner of gold medals at
five consecutive Olympic Games between 1984 and 2000

Using the whole body like this is much harder work, but it multiplies both the *force of each backward rowing stroke* and the equal and opposite *force that drives the boat forward*. For this reason, rowing boats ultimately accelerate and travel *much* faster than canoes or kayaks. In addition, rowing boats can have crews of up to eight rowers working together, which increases the speed even further.

So do two rowers go twice as fast as one, and eight rowers twice as fast as four?

That would seem to make sense, wouldn't it? But, in fact, this doesn't quite happen. This is because of two things. First, every crew member you add also adds weight to the boat. Now because *heavier things take more force to accelerate* (Isaac Newton told us that too), this makes it harder to get the boat up to top speed.

Second, unless the entire crew's oar blades enter and leave the water at *exactly* the same time, then *one rower's oar* will be trying to push the boat forward while *another drags in the water*, slowing the whole boat down.

This is why rowing teams work not only on the power and speed of their strokes, but also on the timing. They try to **match** or **synchronize** the movements of their oar blades as much as possible, minimizing the drag caused by sloppy, poorly timed strokes. To help with this, teams of four or more rowers may also include an extra crew member – the **coxswain**.

The coxswain (or **cox**, for short) sits in the back (or stern) of the boat, facing the rest of the crew, and shouts instructions to help them keep their oar strokes in time. When the cox wants the crew to speed up, he or she makes sure they *all speed up together*. He (or she) also has to be very light, so as not to weigh down the boat too much!

So that person gets to be on the crew, gets to call themselves an athlete, but just sits in the boat *shouting* at people? Awesome! Sounds like my kind of job!

Yeah, but you'd have to diet all the time to keep your weight low, otherwise you'd get the sack.

Oh, so no burgers, then?

Not often, no.

In that case, perhaps I'll keep looking.

Canoeing and Kayaking

How to play

An endurance sport held at indoor pools or outdoor water courses, in which athletes use a single oar (or paddle) to row lightweight canoes or kayaks. Canoes and kayaks race head-to-head in lanes marked by floating buoys, or race around obstacles (and against the clock) in slalom racing events. Canoeists use a short, single-bladed paddle, pulling their boats through the water with rapid strokes on either side. Kayakers use a long, double-bladed paddle to power and steer their craft – using a fluid, rolling paddling motion.

Players
One to four. Canoeists race as individuals or pairs, while kayakers paddle solo or work together in pairs or teams of four to race other boat teams.

Equipment
Canoe – lightweight plastic or carbon fibre shell 3–5m in length. Tapered towards the nose and tail, with gaps in the upper surface (**cockpits**) into which the canoeists slide their legs.

Kayak – plastic/carbon-fibre shell, similar in size and shape to a canoe, but usually narrower across the width. Slalom kayaks are shorter and wider, ideal for tighter turns. Racing kayaks are longer and thinner, and better for straight, flat-water courses.

Paddle – for canoeing, a wide, flat plastic blade mounted on a short (1–1.5m), lightweight wood or aluminium shaft, with a T-shape handle on one end. For kayaking, a 2–3m shaft with rubber handgrips either side of its centre, and a flat plastic blade at each end.

Spray skirt – rubber skirt that stretches from the canoeist or kayaker's waist, and attaches to the upper surface of the canoe, forming a watertight seal over the cockpit. This stops water getting in, which would sink the craft.

Helmet – foam and hard plastic crash helmet that protects the head. Worn in outdoor events to protect the skull from rocks beneath the water surface.

Lifejacket – foam-filled vest that helps the athlete float, should he or she capsize and fall out of the boat.

Cross-country Skiing

How hard would it be to ski UP a mountain?

*Hard. VERY hard. But not impossible. In fact, cross-country skiers ski uphill all the time. It just takes a bit of **knowledge**, a lot of **practice** and almost superhuman levels of **endurance**.*

Really? It'd be *that* hard? Even if you got a good run-up first?

Yep.

Why?

Think about it. What are skis *for*? What do they *do*?

Err . . . you wear them on your feet when you want to travel over snow. They let you zip down snowy slopes really fast.

Right. Long, flat skis increase the **surface area** of your feet. This helps to *spread your body weight* over a *wider area*, which stops you from *sinking* into soft snow.

Eskimo snowshoes (those funny shoes that look a bit like tennis racquets) do this too. But snowshoes have a rough lower surface (made of criss-crossing strings), which *increases friction* and *grips* the snow beneath. Skis, meanwhile, are flatter, narrower and have a *smooth* lower surface that *decreases friction* and slips easily over the snow.

This is wonderful, of course, when you want to travel *downhill*. **Gravity** pulls you downward, and without much *friction* sticking your skis to the slope all you have to do is stay upright and steer. Downhill skiers, then, mostly keep their skis parallel, swivelling their bent knees and leaning their bodies to turn or stop.

Right. Skiing down hills is simple enough. But when you try to ski uphill . . .

. . . then gravity starts to work against you, trying to pull you back down the slope. And the lack of friction you so enjoyed on the way down turns out to be a nightmare on the way up. Without much friction to hold your skis on the slope, they slip several centimetres backwards for every centimetre you ski forward.

So how do cross-country skiers *do* it?

They *increase the friction* in each step by turning the tips of the skis outward and digging the edges of their skis into the snow. Then they **shuffle** (or if it's not too steep, **skate**) up the slope by pushing off from the edge of one ski at a time.

When they reach the top of a hill, they can then happily ski down the other side just like a normal skier would – skis straight and parallel, body and arms tucked in to cut down on **air resistance** and **drag**. On *flat or level plains*, they use one of two methods. They can freestyle it, usually by pushing back and to one side with the inner edges of their skis and **skate** their way forwards. Others keep their skis parallel and shuffle first one ski, then the other. This is called **classic** cross-country skiing.

Which method they use may depend on the type of event (in some races, you're *only* allowed to use the classical method) or the depth of snow (freestyle works well on firm snow, but not too well on very soft snow).

How far can they go like this? You know, like in a proper race?

In the Winter Olympics, cross-country skiers race up to 30 miles (50km) downhill, uphill and across level ground. So, regardless of which techniques the players use, cross-country skiing is still one of the most gruelling sports in the world.

Thirty miles? Whoa! That's like a ski-marathon!

It's *longer* than a marathon. And, just like marathon runners, cross-country skiers have to train for years to build up their **endurance**, just to avoid collapsing in a heap halfway through the race.

In fact, cross-country skiers have the *highest* measured levels of **cardiovascular fitness** *and* **muscular endurance** of any type of athlete.

Cross-country Skiing

How to play
An endurance sport that takes place on snowy outdoor slopes and trails, in which athletes wearing skis and carrying poles race each other over hilly terrain. Unlike most skiers – who only race downhill – cross-country skiers must also make their way uphill and across flat land. To do this, athletes use either a straight, sliding step or a diagonal push-and-glide movement known as **skating** or **freestyling**. Events include the 400m and 1,500m **sprints**, 4 x 10km **relays**, 15km **distance races** and 30-mile (50km) **ski marathons**. The Canadian Ski Marathon is the longest, at an exhausting 160km.

Players
One to four. Most cross-country skiers compete individually, racing against each other or the clock. But in long-distance relay events, teams of four skiers take turns to complete equal portions of the course.

Equipment
Cross-country skis – long, flat strips made of wood, fibreglass and/or plastic polymers, 2–2.3m in length. Nordic skis are longer and narrower than those used in downhill and slalom events, and the tips curve upward more to avoid sticking in the snow. The **bindings** – or **boot clamps** – at the centre of each ski are also a little different. In regular skis, these clamp the whole foot to the surface of the ski. But in cross-country skis, only the toe is fixed, and the boot heel can raise up. This allows Nordic skiers to make the skating motions required for flatland and uphill skiing.

Ski boots – hard plastic, foam-lined boots with locking buckles that secure them on the foot, and plates on the toes, which slide into the **locking bindings** on each ski.

Ski poles – tubular plastic or aluminium poles with hand grips, which help skiers to maintain their balance and propel their movement. Usually a little longer than those used in downhill skiing.

Speed suit – smooth Lycra, one-piece bodysuits that cut down on air resistance and increase speed.

Hang on, aren't endurance and fitness the same thing?

They're related, but not the same. We've already seen how cardio training improves endurance, by improving the ability of your heart and lungs to supply your muscles with oxygen. But there's another part of endurance too – **muscular endurance**. And to be an elite runner, swimmer or cross-country skier, cardiovascular fitness alone is not enough. You also need muscular endurance.

How does that work, then?

Well, during exercise, your muscles not only burn up lots of oxygen, they also create more **toxic waste products** – mostly in the form of **carbon dioxide** and something called **lactic acid** (or **lactate**). Your muscles are *constantly* creating these products as they work – they're like the dirty ash and soot left behind as you burn a pile of logs on a campfire. It's the build-up of lactic acid that makes your muscles hurt when you exercise hard.

For power sports like sprints, jumps and throws, these waste products don't present much of a problem. Although they do build up (and build up fast) during the race, jump or throw, it's all over within a few seconds, and your body can happily remove the built-up wastes as you rest and catch your breath.

But longer races like marathons and ski-marathons require you to keep moving *even while these toxic wastes are building up* in your muscles and bloodstream.

Up to a point, your body can happily keep up with the pace, increasing the rate of waste removal to keep the muscles working well. But, after a while, carbon dioxide and lactic acid begin to build up in the blood, and you reach a point sports scientists call the **lactate threshold**. After this point, athletes **'feel the burn'** and the muscles start to fatigue.

Is that the bit during a long run or swim when your arms and legs start to feel all slow and heavy, like they're made of stone?

Right. Eventually, the muscles become so sore and tired that it becomes a painful effort to keep moving, or even stand up.

Normal people hit this point when they're at about 50% of their **maximum rate of oxygen** uptake (otherwise known as the **VO2 max**). This is what stops most people running more than a mile or two without resting.

But cross-country skiers can hit more than *80% of their maximum oxygen uptake* before their muscles start to get tired. Over many years, endurance training changes the structure of their muscles so that they can *work harder for longer*. It gives them **muscular endurance**.

But how do the muscles change? Do they get bigger?

Not usually, no. In fact, with endurance training, the muscles often become smaller. Endurance is less about the size of the muscle, and more about the types of fibres within.

If you remember, we already met type I (**slow-twitch**) and type II (**fast-twitch**) muscle fibres in chapter one. We found out that fast-twitch muscle fibres use their stored energy quickly, so they're great for *short bursts of power* (like a sprint), but also *tire quickly*.

Slow-twitch muscle fibres do the exact opposite. They use their stored energy more *slowly* and take *much longer to tire out*, so they keep you moving for longer.

For this reason, endurance events rely more upon slow-firing (slow-twitch) muscle fibres, and training for endurance involves *building slow-twitch muscle fibres and energy stores* in the muscles.

Just as power athletes like sprinters, high jumpers and discus throwers try to convert *strength* into *explosive power*, endurance athletes aim to convert *strength* into *muscular endurance*.

So endurance training turns your fast-twitch muscles into slow-twitch ones?

Actually, you can't turn type II muscle fibres into type I fibres. But with proper training, you can *increase the number of new type I fibres in your muscles*, making them better suited to distance events.

What's more, the same training will increase the number of **small blood vessels** (or **capillaries**) that supply each muscle with oxygen, and increase the number and size of

mitochondria (the tiny, energy-converting powerhouses within cells) within each individual muscle cell.

In a sense, endurance training makes you **superhuman**. It turns you into a more *efficient machine*, allowing you to *use less energy* to do the *same amount of work*.

Cool. But, if it's all the same to you, I think I'll stick to skiing *down*hill. Seems like far less effort. And a *lot* more fun . . .

3. He Shoots
... He Scores!

Archery and Shooting

If you're a 'crack shot' with a rifle or a bow and arrow, is that because your eyes are sharper than other people's?

Not necessarily. Although top shooters and archers do tend to have keen eyesight, becoming a 'crack shot' is more about training your brain and nervous system than it is about having sharp eyes. And, in fact, the same thing applies to shooting **basketballs**, **footballs** and **hockey pucks** too.

Eh? What's your brain got to do with shooting arrows and basketballs?

A *lot*, actually. What do you think you're shooting *with*?

Well, your hands . . . and your eyes. You *look* with your eyes, and *shoot* with your hands. Right?

Well, it's true that your eyes take in the image of the target. And your hands aim – and eventually release – the shot. But neither is actually doing the *looking* or *shooting*. The eyes just *relay information* to the **brain**, via the **nervous system**. Your brain then 'sees' the target. This done, the brain *aims the shot* by sending signals to the muscles in your hands, again, via the **nervous system**.

Shooting anything, whether it's an arrow, basketball or hockey puck, requires what is commonly called hand-eye coordination. But, in reality, the thing that coordinates the eyes and hands is the **nervous system**. So learning to shoot means *training* your nervous system.

Oh. Didn't really think of it like that. So what makes up your nervous system, then, and what does it do?

Your **nervous system** includes your **brain**, **spinal cord** and **nerves**. Together, these form a **high-speed communication system** that *controls and connects* every organ and tissue. It's like the body's very own internet.

Really?

Yep. And, just like the internet, the nervous system can be used for lots of different things.

Like what?

Well, for starters, you can use the

NERVOUS SYSTEM

internet to send and receive messages, store and save memories (in the form of digital documents, pictures and video clips), work, chat, learn, play games and much, much more.

Similarly, your nervous system sends and receives messages between muscles and organs via the **nerves**, stores and saves memories in the **brain**, and *coordinates thought, speech, learning and movement.*

But *unlike* the internet, which has no single controller, for most purposes, the brain is the 'big boss' of the nervous system.

The list of things for which you can use your brain and nervous system is almost limitless. But here we're going to keep it simple. For the purposes of sport and exercise, it has three basic functions: **moving**, **sensing** and **interpreting**.

We'll learn more about each of these in the next section. But even without knowing about these things in detail we can see right away how you can use your nervous system to shoot, and learn to shoot *better*.

How's that?

It's quite simple, really. Learning to shoot means *sensing* (or looking at) a target, then *moving* your hands into the correct position (aiming) and taking the shot. Then you *look again* to see where your shot ended up, or by how much you missed the target. Armed with this new image, your brain can then *interpret* (or make sense of) that information, and figure out which way to adjust your aiming movements before shooting again. Then you *shoot again*, *observe* the result, *interpret* the information, correct your aim, and on and on it goes.

Shooting, then, is about training yourself to *miss by less* with every shot, using these three processes of *sensing, moving* and *interpreting*. The more you practise, the smaller the distance you miss by, and the smaller the adjustment you have to make to your aiming movements. Or as the sharp-shooting cowboys of the old

American West used to put it: 'Aim small, miss small.'

Archery

How to play
An individual or team game played on long indoor or outdoor archery ranges, in which players with bows shoot arrows into circular targets. The targets are positioned at various ranges or distances, and depending on the type of event players may have to shoot at one range or several.

Points are scored for every hit on the target, with hits closer to the centre scoring highest. Points are added, and the player or team with the highest score wins.

Archery competitions are played in rounds, with each archer getting three to six shots (or arrows) per round. Each shot can score a maximum of 10 points, depending on how close to the centre (or inner bullseye) the arrow strikes. There are five coloured scoring zones on each target – each one subdivided into two halves (inner and outer).

They are scored as follows (arranged from outer edge to the centre):

White   1–2 points (1 point for **outer white**, 2 points for **inner white**)

Black   3–4 points

Blue   5–6 points

Red   7–8 points

Gold   9–10 points (10 points – or **inner gold** – being the bullseye)

In the Olympic Games, athletes shoot from a distance of 70m. The tournament is played in a knockout format over five sets. Each set consists of three arrows being fired. The winners of each match move on to the next round.

Players

In **individual archery**, players compete solo.

In **team archery**, teams of three players compete, adding their scores for the win.

Equipment

Bow – most modern archers use **recurve bows** around 1.5m long, made of wood, fibreglass and/or carbon fibre.

The tips of the bow (which hold the ends of the high-tension, synthetic-fibre bowstring) bend away from the archer, increasing the spring in the bow for more powerful and accurate shooting. Most modern bows also have metal **balancing rods** which stick out of the bow forward* or sideways to help keep the bow level and stable, along with eye-level **sighting rods** or viewfinders that assist aiming.

Arrows – made of wood, aluminium or carbon fibre, with an adjustable tip, plastic fletching (where the feathered flights would have been in the past) to help the arrow fly straight, and a V-shaped notch (or **nock**) in a rear end, into which the **bowstring** fits.

Targets – usually circular 'bullseye'-type targets made from coiled straw ropes, measuring 80–120cm across. Olympic archery targets are 122cm in diameter, with the gold ring at the centre (worth a maximum 10 points) measuring just 12.2cm. The centre of the target is raised about 1.2m off the ground by mounting the target on a three-legged metal frame.

Forearm and chest guards – also known as **bracers**. Strapped on to the inside of the forward arm, and across the leading side of the chest (usually the left side). These protect the skin from friction burns caused by the whipping bowstring.

Finger tabs – leather finger guards worn over the fingers of the drawing hand. These stop the high-tension bowstring from cutting into the skin after many draws.

---

* Making it look as if another archer has shot an arrow into the bow from the front!

But how does that help in an archery tournament? I mean, if you keep missing the bullseye, won't you lose the match before you figure out how to hit it?

The idea is that you practise enough beforehand so that your nervous system *already knows* how to hit the bullseye at a given distance, even before you start the tournament. Besides, it's not necessary to hit the bullseye *every time* to win an archery competition. At long range, even Olympic archers have trouble doing that.

Plus, since the archers shoot batches of three arrows, one after the other, even if the first arrow goes off-target they can use the *visual information* from the first shot to *adjust* their aim and get *closer* to the bullseye with the next two.

It's a Bullseye! The term 'bullseye' dates back to the seventeenth century, when it was used to describe any small, circular object – including coins, sweets and small, round windows set into the lower decks of ships. By 1830, it had been adopted by archers and darts players to describe the centre of the target. Thankfully, it seems that no real bulls were harmed in the making of this phrase . . .

Olympic shooting competitors train in a similar way. Expert pistol and rifle shooters usually specialize at shooting targets set at one particular distance, using one particular type of pistol or rifle. So, in training, a 50m pistol expert will use a 50m air pistol to shoot at a target 50m away, over and over again. A 300m rifle shooter, meanwhile, will use a .22 long rifle to shoot at targets exactly 300m away.

Besides that, the process of training the nervous system is the same as in archery: **aim**, **shoot**, **observe**, **interpret**, **adjust** and repeat. Lately, though, some archers and shooters have begun using a high-tech method called **neurofeedback training** to gain an edge over their competitors. This involves training their **brains** and **emotional states** as well as their **sense of aim**.

Brain-training? How does that work, then?

Neurofeedback training, also known as **biofeedback training**, involves connecting the trainee to a machine that measures brainwaves, called an **electroencephalogram** (or **EEG,** for short). This machine measures brainwaves in the brain's **motor cortex** region – the part of the brain that controls the physical movements (more on that later).

The trainee is hooked up to the EEG machine by placing sticky electrodes on the temples and forehead, which pick up electrical activity in the wearer's brain, otherwise known as **brainwaves**. Among these is a special pattern of brainwaves called the **sensorimotor rhythm**, or **SMR**. This particular pattern of waves gets *bigger* when the body is *still*, and *smaller* when one or more parts of the body are *moving*.

In neurofeedback training, the EEG sensor is attached to a computer which shows the athlete their SMR brainwaves in action. Usually, this is in the form of a coloured column on a computer screen. As the size of the SMR brainwaves *increases*, the column *grows* in size. As the SMR brainwaves *decrease*, the column *shrinks*.

Hooked up this way, athletes can see their brainwaves in action, and see how their nervous state affects their bodies. Then they can practise controlling their nervous state, by playing a brain-training game. If they're excited or nervous, the column on the screen shrinks. But as they calm their minds and bodies, the column on the screen grows. So the goal is to be as calm as possible, and make the on-screen column grow taller. When the column passes a certain height, the athlete is rewarded with a ringing bell sound, or a brightly coloured star shape on screen.

Shooting

How to play
An individual or team game played on outdoor shooting ranges in which players use air pistols, rifles or shotguns to hit static or moving targets. In **pistol and rifle shooting**, players try to get as many shots on target within a fixed time limit. As in archery, shots closer to the centre of the circular target score more points. In **shotgun** (or **trap**) **shooting**, players shoot at flying clay discs, launched from two mechanical catapults called **traps**. In **single-trap** shooting, the clays are launched one at a time, with a three-second delay in between. In **double-trap** (or **skeet**) shooting, two clays are launched simultaneously from opposite sides of the field, and the shooter gets one shot at each. Hits (which need not obliterate the clay target, but must at least chip a piece off it) score one point, while misses score zero.

Players
In **individual shooting**, players compete solo.

In **team shooting**, teams of three to five players compete, adding their scores for the win.

Equipment

Air pistol – different types of air pistol are used for each range and event type. But all use compressed air or carbon dioxide to shoot small lead or plastic pellets. Most have moulded plastic grips to assist in holding the gun with one hand.

Air rifle – as with air pistols, these shoot small lead pellets using compressed gases. But air rifles have a much longer range and pellet speed, along with a telescopic sight for more accurate aiming over distance.

.22 rifle – these long wood/metal rifles shoot .22-calibre lead cartridges, much like those used in hunting. They also have barrel-mounted sights or viewfinders, and a special palm rest for supporting the weight of the rifle with the forward hand.

12-gauge shotgun – used in trap shooting, these wood/metal shotguns have two barrels (arranged over and under, rather than side by side) for shooting pairs of flying targets without reloading. They shoot buckshot (lead pellet) cartridges that scatter a little as they fly, giving more chance of hitting a moving target.

Targets – for pistol and rifle shooting, 30cm circular paper targets are used, similar to those used in archery, only smaller. For trap shooting, 11cm-wide, saucer-shaped clay targets are used.

Trap – adjustable, voice-activated mechanical catapult, which flings clay targets over 60m through the air. A single trap can hold up to 400 clays.

OK . . . so how does all that help someone learn to aim or shoot?

Precise (or **fine**) **motor skills** like aiming and shooting are easily disturbed when you're nervous or excited. Excitement and fear create excess tension in the muscles, which results in twitchy, uneven movements. This makes it difficult to do the fine-tuned movement required to aim an arrow or bullet a millimetre or so to the left or right of where the last shot hit.

The calmer you are, the more accurate your aim. Think of a cat just before it pounces on a mouse. Having sneaked into a pouncing range, the cat takes a second or two to stay perfectly still, calm itself and ready itself to strike. Then it launches itself at the mouse with deadly accuracy.*

But in world championship competitions like the Olympics, athletes representing their countries have just *one chance* to succeed, after years and years of training. As you might imagine, that makes most competitors anything but calm by the time they reach the finals.

Many sports scientists believe that by learning to control their SMR brainwaves athletes can learn to *calm their minds* during intense sporting competitions, and instantly improve their accuracy and performance.

Does that really work?

Well, in 2011, a team of Indian scientists took a group of twenty-four archers, trained half of them using a neurofeedback brain-trainer, and left the other half to themselves. After just twelve training sessions, the group that did the neurofeedback training performed much

---

* The average domestic cat can pounce so precisely that they can bury the tip of one tooth between a mouse's neckbones (or vertebrae), which are less than half a millimetre apart. Now *that's* accurate.

better than those who did not – *shooting more accurately* and *scoring much higher* in the contest held at the end of the experiment.

Not all scientists are convinced by neurofeedback training yet. But some believe it will change the way elite athletes train forever. Not just archers, but also swimmers, soccer players, skiers . . . everybody.

Coooool.

Of course, if you want to take up this sport, you have to make sure you do it safely, as guns – even air pistols – can be very dangerous. So the best way to do it is to join a shooting club, where experienced instructors can show you how to shoot targets safely.

But if you want to have a go at improving your aim you don't even need an air pistol to do it. Try the exercise opposite, and you'll be a 'crack shot' in no time!

Give it a go!

Exercise: aim small, miss small
Type: skill
Goal: improving your aim

1. Draw a circular, archery-style target on a wall in chalk, or draw one on a large piece of cardboard and tape it to the wall.
2. Grab a tennis ball, walk at least five metres away from the wall and chalk a line on the ground. This is your shooting line, and you're not allowed to put a foot beyond it.
3. Now take aim and throw, trying to hit the very centre of the target. Watch where it hits. (This will be easier if you chalked the target, as this bit will smudge.)
4. If the ball went high, aim a little lower than the centre next time. If it went to the left, aim a little to the right. But don't overdo it – just aim a few centimetres away from the centre, in the opposite direction to where your last shot hit.
5. Now throw again, look again and adjust your aim just a little bit.
6. Repeat at least fifty times. This done, take a break, then repeat every day for a week! I guarantee you'll be a much better shot by the following week.

You can also try this with a football, or with a tennis racquet and ball. It all depends which sport (and what kind of shot) you're interested in improving.

Now get some friends together and see how they fare against you!

Basketball, Netball and Volleyball

How do basketball players 'hang' in the air when they do a jumping slam dunk?

They don't. No matter how high they leap, basketball players cannot hover or fly. Like everybody else, they start falling back down immediately after they jump up. Gravity makes sure of that. It only looks like they 'hang' in the air because they're moving forward as well as upward.

But when you see them on TV they seem to stay in the air for *ages*. If I jump up, I plop back to the ground again right away.

Well, most professional basketball players (at least the ones who play in attacking positions) can jump pretty high. So they probably get a bit more time in the air than you on the average jump. But we're only talking about fractions of a second. No matter how high you jump, you can't fight the ever-present force of **gravity**. Humans simply cannot hover. At least, not without a jet pack . . .

. . . or rocket-powered trainers.

Right. If they even existed. Which they don't.

That would be awesome, though.

Yes. It would.

So why does it look like the players are hovering when they're not?

It's a trick of the eyes (or, more accurately, the brain) which makes it hard to judge how long they stay in the air.

I don't get it.

Look at it this way: if a player jumps straight up, all his **velocity** (a combination of speed and direction) is **vertical**. He accelerates *upward* at the start of the jump, but since gravity is constantly pulling him *downward*, his jump velocity starts *slowing* immediately, and he reaches a peak of maybe just over a metre off the ground.

Then he comes *straight* back down again, and we clearly see how that upward velocity has been lost, and transferred into downward velocity. The whole thing takes just under a second to happen.

We're *used* to seeing this kind of thing. Toss an apple or tennis ball in the air and it slows, reverses direction and comes down again. What goes up must come down. Simple.

Basketball

How to play
A team game played on a large indoor or outdoor court. Players throw, catch, bounce and dribble* a large rubber ball with their hands. Points are scored by passing the ball through netted hoops found at each end of the court, mounted on poles or walls to a height of 3m.**

Players
Ten – two teams, five a side.

Equipment
Basketball – 75cm in circumference, made of heavy rubber and/or synthetic leather. Weighs about half a kilo. Hurts when it hits you in the face.
Baskets – mounted at a height of 3m, with a wooden or plexiglass backboard for missed and rebounding shots.

Rules
Each team is assigned to one half of the court, and aims to shoot into the basket at the opposite end. Play begins with a 'jump ball' in the middle of the court (otherwise known as 'half court'), in which two opposing players leap to catch the ball, lobbed skyward by the referee. Thereafter, players try to run (dribble), pass or shoot the ball around opposing players to reach the target basket. But here's the kicker: you can only use one hand at a time to dribble, meaning

---

* Dribble, in this sense, means 'move with the ball, around other players', as opposed to 'drool on the ball/other players/referee'. Getting this wrong could prove very embarrassing.
** Thus, in basketball, it helps if you're (a) tall, (b) a good jumper or (c) *both*.

you have to bounce it with one hand while you move. Once you stop bouncing the ball and take it in both hands, you can't move any further – you can only pass or shoot.

Teams score points, of course, by shooting or dunking the ball into the basket. If the ball is tossed in from behind an arced line (the three-point line) roughly 6.5m from the basket, the shot scores three points. If it's shot or dunked from a position inside this line, it only scores two. Fouls (running with the ball in two hands, elbowing other players in the face) result in losing possession or earn you free shots at the basket, which earn one point each.

The game is played in four fifteen-minute quarters.

OK . . .

But when a basketball player takes a running leap towards the net for a slam dunk, he doesn't travel up and down in a straight line. He has **horizontal velocity** (or forward motion) as well as **vertical velocity** (or upward motion).

Because of this, his path through the air is not a straight line, but an arc. When a player is moving forward as well as upward like this, it's harder for our eyes and brains to separate the horizontal and vertical speeds, and harder to recognize how long it takes for the player to reach the top of his jump.

In reality, gravity affects the vertical part of this jump in exactly the same way as it did when the player jumped straight up. He goes up and comes down in less than a second, just as before. But, since the player spends up to half of that second in the top part of the arc, it appears as if he spends at least a quarter of a second hovering in the air, in what basketball fans call 'hang time'.

Slow the whole thing down in an **action replay**, and you'll see that the player starts falling as soon as he's finished accelerating upward. So, in reality, there is no 'hang'.

Why *do* they jump up like that to shoot, anyway? Seems like a lot of effort. Why not just toss it into the basket with their feet on the ground?

Well, if you can pull it off, jumping at the basket and simply *placing* the ball through the hoop is a *lot* easier than trying to *toss* the ball into the hoop with a well-aimed, arcing throw. In fact, even when they shoot from a distance, basketball players will often still jump up straight before shooting, as it allows the ball to *approach the hoop at a higher angle*. This reduces the chances of the ball bouncing off the rim of the hoop, and increases the chances that it'll drop through instead.*

---

* If you want to learn how to take the perfect basketball jump-shot, see the exercise on page 136.

Netball

How to play
A team game, similar to basketball, in which players throw and catch a large ball, and score points by shooting it through a high hoop. But in netball you're not allowed to run (or dribble) while holding the ball.

Players
Fourteen. Two teams, seven a side.

Equipment
Netball – smaller and lighter than a basketball.
Goals – metal hoops or rings (with or without* net) mounted atop 3m poles, with no backboard.

Rules
Play begins at centre-court, with one team's centre player passing the ball to another player on their team. From there, both teams try to intercept passes and shoot at the other's goal. Once they have the ball, players are not allowed to take more than one step. So netball players use crafty, agile footwork to move into positions where they can make or receive passes – or shoot at the goal – without being blocked or intercepted. Shots can *only* be taken from inside the 'shooting circle' – a 5m semicircle centred on each goal ring. All successful shots score one point.

The game is played in four fifteen-minute quarters.

---

* Confusingly, no one calls it 'ring ball' or 'hoop ball'. Even when there's no net present, it's still 'netball'. Weird.

So why don't netball players jump or slam dunk the ball, then? Wouldn't it make their shots more accurate too?

It would, but the rules of netball are different. In netball, players are not allowed to move or jump once they have the ball. They can jump to *catch* the ball. But once it's caught, they have to keep at least one foot on the ground at all times. So jump-shots are a no-no.

No Dunks, Please Slam dunking, or jumping at a basketball hoop and slamming the ball down through it, first appeared in the 1940s, with 7-foot-tall American Olympic gold medallist Bob Kurland. It was banned in US games between 1967 and 1976, but later allowed under new rules. The phrase 'slam dunk' has now become a popular phrase, meaning 'can't miss' or 'guaranteed'.

Harsh.

A bit, yes. Jump-shots are common in other team ball games, though.

In the faster, rougher game of **handball**, the goal is not a high hoop, but a square net with a goalkeeper, similar to those seen in five-a-side football.

Like netball players, handball players aren't permitted to run once they have the ball. Nor are they allowed to shoot from too close to the goal, which is surrounded by a 6m-wide semicircular 'no-go-zone' called the **crease**.

Since they can't run into this to shoot, handball players often jump into it instead. Provided the shot goes in before they land, the goal is counted. Plus the jump allows the player to fire the shot *downward* at the goalie's feet, making it faster and harder to catch.

Now *that* sounds like my kind of game. BAM! Take that, goalie! Bwahahahahaaaa!
Indeed.

Don't volleyball players jump and smash like that too?
Right. In **volleyball**, the jumping smash-shot (or **spike**) is the most common way to win a point. Without jumping up to meet the ball in the air, it's pretty much impossible to whack the ball downward over the high net that separates the two halves of a volleyball court.

Handball

How to play
A team game played like a cross between netball and soccer, in which players dribble, throw, catch, smash and shoot a large ball, scoring points by shooting it through football-like goals (complete with keeper) at either end of an indoor court. Like netball, you're not allowed to run (or dribble) while holding the ball. But in handball you can touch the ball with any part of the body above the knee, which makes for a faster, rougher game.

Players
Fourteen. Two teams, seven a side. Six '**outfielders**' plus one **goalkeeper** on each team.

Equipment

Handball – smaller and lighter than a basketball, roughly the same size and weight as a netball.

Goals – netted frames measuring about 3m x 2m, like soccer goals, only smaller.

Gloves – some players wear these to improve grip, while others use a sticky resin on their bare hands.

Rules

Play begins at centre-court, with a 'throw off', or pass from a centre player to one of his own team. From there, both teams try to intercept passes and shoot at the other's goal. Players are not allowed to hold the ball for more than three seconds and can't take more than three steps while holding the ball, so have to dribble (or bounce) the ball, as in basketball. But, once stopped, they get another three steps before they have to shoot or pass. In contrast to netball, shots can only be taken from *outside* the shooting zone (known as the **crease**) – a 6m semicircle centred on each goal. But players are allowed to leap over the crease line and shoot in mid-air.* A goal scores one point. The teams with the most goals at the end of the match wins.

The game is played in two thirty-minute halves.

---

* Which is, of course, enormous fun for the shooter, but terrifying for the poor goalie.

Must be pretty tough to do, though. I mean, first you have to time your jump, then you have to aim your shot in mid-air . . .

Right. And you've only got about half a second to do both. This goes for *any* jumping shot, whether it's in basketball, handball or volleyball.

How do you learn it, then?

The same way that you learn to shoot a rifle or bow and arrow: **shoot**, **observe**, **correct** and **repeat**, until your brain and body make timing and performing jump-shots almost automatic, and the whole series of movements gets embedded in your **muscle memory**.

More on how that works later on.

For now, have a go at the shot-training drill on the next page, and impress your friends with your newfound shooting skills!

Give it a go!

Exercise: the perfect free throw
Type: skill
Goal: improving your basketball shooting skills

1. Go to a school gym or public sports centre, grab a basketball and find a hoop to shoot at.
2. Stand on the free-throw spot, marked on the court in front on the hoop, and hold the ball over your forehead – one hand (your right hand if right-handed) beneath the ball, the other on the side.
3. Aim for a spot *just above the back of the hoop*. Don't aim for the centre of the hoop. Scientists have shown that this decreases your chances of making the shot by 3% or more.
4. Jump into the air just before shooting to get a better angle on the net.
5. At the top of your jump, push the ball with your lower hand, releasing it at a 45–50° angle. Try to put some **backspin** on the ball by letting it roll off the tips of your fingers as you release. This will deaden the bounce as it hits the backboard, decreasing the chances of it 'bouncing out' if you're a little off-target. It's a sure-fire way of making your shot 'lucky'!
6. Watch where the ball goes, and adjust your aim for the next shot accordingly. If it went too far left, aim a little to the right, and vice versa. But always aim at the back of the hoop.
7. Repeat until brilliant. Challenge your friends. Join the school basketball team.
8. Make huge money as a professional basketball player in America. Remember who taught you to shoot, and send me lots of cash.

Volleyball

How to play

A team game played across a high, wide net in the centre of an indoor or outdoor court. Players strike the ball with their hands, fists or forearms, and score points by landing (or 'grounding') the ball in the opposing team's half of the court.

Players

For standard volleyball, twelve on court: two teams of six per side. For beach volleyball, four players on court: two teams of two per side.

Equipment

Volleyball – small leather/synthetic ball: about half the size and weight of a basketball.

Net – 9m across, 1m high, with the top set at a height of 2.4m.

Rules

Play begins with one player serving the ball over the net, as in tennis (only without the racquet). The receiving team's players then try to keep the ball aloft and send it back over the net. Each team only has three hits in which to get the ball back over the net. If the same player touches the ball two times in a row, then their team loses a point, likewise if they catch the ball, miss the ball or knock it out of the court. Points are typically scored by one player 'setting' the ball (i.e. lifting the ball over the head of a teammate close to the net), and another 'spiking' (or smashing) it downward into the opposing court with an open hand.

Racquet Sports

Why do tennis racquets have strings?

*The strings on a tennis, squash or badminton racquet add power to your shots, by **storing and releasing energy**. As the strings rebound, that energy is transferred to the ball or shuttle, which rockets off far faster than it would from a solid bat or paddle.*

Tennis racquets can store energy? I didn't know that. Do they have batteries in them or something?

Err . . . no – they don't. We're not talking about *that* kind of energy. Batteries store **chemical** energy that can be converted into **electricity**. Tennis racquets, on the other hand, store (for a fraction of a second) **potential** energy in the form of **elastic tension**. Then they release this energy back to the ball as it bounces free.

I don't get it.

Here's how it works. As the ball hits the racquet, it transfers some of the energy of its movement (or **kinetic energy**) to the strings. In response, the strings bend, flex and tighten, and **energy** builds within them. **Elastic potential energy**, to be precise. As the strings rebound, they transfer this energy back into the ball – plus a little extra 'zip' provided by the swing you gave the racquet in the first place.*

When the ball bounces free of the racquet, then, it not only has energy from your muscular swing, but also part of the energy that it *approached* you with – *stored* and *rereleased* by the strings of the tennis racquet.

So why do you need strings to do that? Wouldn't a solid bat work just as well? Seems to work well enough in cricket and baseball . . .

Not quite, no. While solid bats also bend and spring back a little, storing and releasing part of the energy of an approaching ball, they also deform (or squash) the ball more as they do so.

This is fine if you're using a cricket ball or baseball, as they're very hard, and don't squash very easily. But when you hit a softer, squishier tennis ball with a solid bat the ball squashes too much on impact, and around *half* of its moving (kinetic) energy will be lost. Or, rather, converted into **friction** and **heat** as the ball squashes up.

Strings help prevent this by bending around the softer ball, allowing it to *hold on to its shape* (and kinetic energy) a little better. This is why top tennis players avoid making the strings on their racquets too tight. If the strings don't bend enough, they squash the ball, and it won't rebound with as much speed. String your racquet a little looser, and the ball will actually go faster.

---

* This energy is also, of course, transferred via the strings. It goes from your moving muscles, through the moving frame of the tennis racquet and into the strings attached to it.

Tennis

How to play

A two- or four-player ball game in which players hit a small, bouncy ball between two halves of a large court, divided by a central net. The ball must bounce (or at least be on target to do so) within your opponent's area to remain in play. If it bounces twice – or your opponent fails to return it after one bounce – you win the point. But if it bounces more than once in *your* area then *you* lose the point. Simple, really.

Players

For singles matches, two players play head-to-head.

For doubles matches, four players battle it out two a side.

Equipment

Tennis ball – small (6.7cm diameter), light, rubber ball filled with air (which makes it bouncy) and covered in white or yellow felt (which reduces drag and helps it to fly faster and straighter).

Racquet – wooden, metal or carbon-fibre frame mounted on a gripped handle. The frame is strung with criss-crossing nylon strings, which bend and accelerate the ball on contact.

Net – 0.9m high, stretched across the width of the 8–11m court.

Scoring

Scoring can get a bit complicated, but basically winning four

points* will win you a **game**, winning at least six games – or two more games than your opponent – will win you a **set**. The entire **match** is won by winning more than half of the sets. The total number of sets differs in men's and women's tennis. Men's matches are played 'best out of five',** while women's are played 'best out of three'. (Doubles matches, too, are usually played 'best out of three'.)

The game is played until someone wins, with no specific time limit.***

So do squash racquets and badminton racquets have strings for the same reason?

Yep – same reason.

Squash balls are smaller and squishier than tennis balls. They come in a variety of different types with different 'speed' and 'bounce' characteristics. Again, the **strings** on a squash racquet help to ensure that the squash ball doesn't lose too much energy on impact. But, in fact, expert squash players actually prefer *slower, less bouncy* balls, anyway, as they get more *control* over its flight and bounce. This is very important in squash, because it's a very different game to tennis.

---

* Just to add confusion, the points don't go up one at a time, either. The score starts at 0–0 (or 'love-all'). The first winning point takes you to 15–0 ('fifteen love'), the second to 30–0 ('thirty love'), the third to 40–0 ('forty love') and the fifth wins the game outright ('game'). Other scores, like 40–40 ('deuce') complicate things further, as players must then win another 'advantage' point, then one more to win the game. If you want someone to blame for all this, it's the French. They nicked the game from the ancient Egyptians, Greeks and Romans, then added their own crazy scoring system.

** There's an added rule, though, that if the set score goes to 2–2, you have to get two games ahead in order to win the fifth set. Hence, if you don't win 3–0 or 3–1, then you have to win 6–4, 7–5 or 8–6 (and so on) in that final set, depending on how many times your opponent draws level with you.

*** Put this together with the rule above, and you can see why some men's tennis matches go on for *several hours*, or even *days*. The longest to date took over eleven hours, played over the course of three days, and ended in a score for the final set of 70–68!

How so?

Well, in tennis, play begins with one player **serving** (or hitting) the ball over the net and into the opponent's court. From there, the ball is hit back and forth until someone fails to return it or hits it out of the court. Players then aim to hit the ball into areas from which the opponent will find it difficult or impossible to hit back. But in top-level tennis the serves are so fast and powerful that back-and-forth **rallies** only happen once in a while.

Really? How fast does a tennis serve go?

As of January 2012, the fastest tennis serve ever recorded clocked in at an incredible **156mph** (251km/h). At Wimbledon, top tennis players *frequently* hit serves that rocket past the net at **130mph** (210km/h) or more.

Yikes! It's a wonder that any of them are hit back at all!

Right. That's why shot speed and power is such a big deal in tennis. But in **squash** and **badminton**, accuracy and control are more important.

A squash game begins just like a tennis game – with one player **serving** the ball into the opponent's area, and the other player attempting to **return** it. But in squash the player stands in a specific 'service box' on one side, and the service has to bounce off the front wall (*above* a marked 'service' line about a third of the way up), below the 'out' line, and land within the **quarter court** on the opposite side. From there, the ball is smashed back and forth against the wall (and into any area of the floor) until someone fails to return it to the wall before **two** bounces, or hits it above any of the marked 'out' lines.

As in tennis, squash players aim to hit the ball into areas from which the opponent will find it difficult to return – like the front of the court if the opponent is at the back, or vice versa. But, with the added complication of walls, the landing spot of the rocketing squash ball is much harder to read. So how *hard* you hit the ball is less important than where you place it, or how awkward a shot is to hit back. A popular winning tactic is to bounce the ball into a **back corner** of the court and make the bounce 'die' with two quick rebounds there. It's almost *impossible* to return the ball from this position.

Squash

How to play
A two- or four-player game in which players hit a small bouncy rubber ball against the hard walls of an indoor court. The ball must hit the main (or front) wall at least once to remain in play, and cannot bounce above the 'out' lines marked on each of the four walls. After hitting one or more walls, the ball may bounce on the floor once. But if it bounces twice, or your opponent fails to return it after one bounce, you win the point. It's a bit like crazy, high-speed tennis played in a small room.*

Players
For singles matches, two players play head-to-head, standing side by side.

For doubles matches (rarer), four players battle it out two a side (two on the left, two on the right).

Equipment
Ball – a hollow, air-filled, rubber ball around 40mm in diameter. Squash balls are *very* fast, and *very* bouncy.

Racquet – wooden, metal or carbon-fibre frame mounted on a gripped handle, strung with criss-crossing nylon strings. Like a tennis racquet, only with a smaller head and a longer handle. This makes hitting a fast-moving squash ball harder, but ensures that the ball really *zings* when it does.

Court – this is the important bit. A squash court is a walled box 9.75m long, 6.4m wide, with walls at least 4.6m high.

---

* Basically, everything your mum told you *not* to do when you were little. Which is part of what makes it so much fun.

The back wall, though, has an 'out' line painted at a height of 2.2m, and the side walls are marked with diagonal 'out' lines that trail from 4.6m at the front corners to 2.2m at the back corners. The court floor is divided in half, front to back with a service line, and the back half divided further into smaller 'quarter courts' and 'service boxes' used during the service portion of the game.

Scoring
Games are scored in single points, the game being won by the first player to reach nine, eleven or twenty-one points (depending on the match type). Matches are played to the best out of five games, and neither games nor matches have any set time limit.

Sneaky. What about badminton?

Badminton can be even sneakier. Again, badminton players aim to hit the shuttle into areas from which the opponent will find it difficult or impossible to hit back, and the strings on a badminton racquet help transfer energy to the shuttle for more powerful shots. But, like squash, badminton is more about **tactics** than raw power.

Winning tactics include (a) driving your opponent to the back of his court, then playing a quick, near-net '**drop shot**' that he has no hope of reaching, and (b) forcing your opponent to lift the shuttle with an awkward return, so that you can leap into the air and **smash** it mercilessly to the ground in his (or her) court area.*

---

* This is the moment most badminton players live for. You can see the evil glee on their faces as they let it rip. Some even aim at their opponents' bodies!

So which game is the fastest: tennis, squash or badminton?

Well, while tennis balls tend to arrive at the **highest speeds**, squash and badminton are played on smaller courts, over shorter distances. Tennis balls, squash balls and badminton shuttles all travel at over 100mph (140km/h) when smashed hard enough. But squash and badminton games *look* and *feel* faster because the opposing players are closer together, so have to react faster to return each shot.

The same thing goes for **table tennis** (also known as **ping-pong**). Here, the 'court' area is very small, and the players very close. So, even if the ball doesn't hit the 130mph of a top tennis serve, it feels like it's going *even faster*, and you'll have difficulty returning shots at even **half** that speed.

Is that why table tennis bats don't have strings? To slow the ball down a bit?

That's part of it, yes. The tiny air-filled table-tennis balls are much lighter than those used in tennis, or even squash. They actually travel *very fast over short distances*, but *lose speed over long distances*, due to air resistance. So stringed bats wouldn't help much, as the ball already goes fast enough for this short-range game.

But the rubber-coated solid **bats** (or **paddles**) are also used because they **grip** the smooth, slippery ball better than strings, allowing the player to add more **spin** to the ball. In tennis, the hardest, fastest serves and shots are usually the ones that get past an opponent. But in table tennis, the winning shots are usually those with the trickiest **spin** and **bounce**.

So, in practice, ping-pong players spend less time whacking *fast* shots across the table, and more time putting *spin* on the ball (typically by chopping at it with the paddle at an angle) so that it bounces in unexpected ways. **Top-spin** can send a

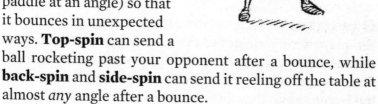

ball rocketing past your opponent after a bounce, while **back-spin** and **side-spin** can send it reeling off the table at almost *any* angle after a bounce.

How can you *ever* learn to hit a shot like that? I mean, it's coming so fast, it seems like you wouldn't have time to think.

Actually, you don't. Top players in all four of these sports practise until their returns become almost automatic. When a top squash or badminton player dives at a smash to prevent it hitting the floor, he or she isn't really *thinking* at all.

But I thought you said earlier that your brain and nerves controlled all your movements and responses.

They do. But that doesn't mean the brain has to *think* to do it. Here's how it all fits together . . .

As we've already discovered, one basic function of your

nervous system is to control movement. To do this, it *relays signals from the brain to the muscles, telling them to contract.*

The bit of the brain that controls muscle movement is called the **motor cortex**. This region sits on the top edge of the brain, in a broad stripe that runs around the middle of the brain like a girl's hairband. Each *part of the motor cortex* controls muscles in a *specific part of the body* – there are regions that relate to the hand muscles, foot muscles, facial muscles, and everything in between.

OK. That makes sense, I s'pose.

This is where your **nerves** come in. Signals travel from the motor cortex to the muscles through **motor nerves** or **motor neurons**. One end of each motor neuron lies in the brain, while the other attaches to a group of **muscle fibres** within a muscle. The longest motor neurons – the ones that run from the brain to the muscles in the toes – can measure over *2m* long!

One motor neuron may attach to as few as five or as many as 1,000 muscle fibres. Together, a single neuron and its fibres form one **motor unit**. Firing a signal through it will make every muscle fibre in the motor unit contract at once.

By coordinating the firing of different motor units, *the brain controls every kind of movement* your body can make. One set of signals might bend a single index finger. Another will wrap all five fingers round the grip of a tennis racquet. Yet **another** will angle and swing an arm to deliver a powerful cross-court tennis serve that screams past your opponent at over 150mph.

Badminton

How to play

A two- or four-player game in which players hit a small, feathered missile (known as a **shuttlecock**, or simply **shuttle**) between two halves of a court divided by a high, central net. As in tennis, the shuttle must land (or at least threaten to land) within your opponents' area to remain in play. But, unlike balls, shuttles don't bounce. So, if the shuttle actually *lands*, a point is won. If it lands in your opponent's area, you win the point. If it lands in *your* area, *you* lose the point. In many ways, this makes badminton even simpler than tennis. But, because the shuttle must be kept aloft, this also makes the game faster and more frantic.

Players

For singles matches, two players play head-to-head.

For doubles matches, four players battle it out two-a-side.

Equipment

Shuttle – sixteen overlapping feathers (often synthetic), embedded in a small cork hemisphere.

Racquet – metal or carbon-fibre frame mounted on a gripped handle. The frame is strung with criss-crossing nylon strings, which bend to accelerate the shuttle on contact. Smaller, lighter and more flexible than a tennis racquet, allowing for faster swings and smashes.

Net – 1.5m high, stretched across the width of the 6.1m court.

Scoring

Scoring, thankfully, is much simpler than in tennis. Twenty-one points win you the game, and matches are played to the best of three games. The game is played until someone wins, with no specific time limit.

So that's how you *hit* a 150mph serve. But that doesn't explain how you can hit one *back*.

Right. Returning a serve relies heavily on the *second* major function of your nervous system – **sensing**.

In addition to telling your body how to move, your nervous system also *relays signals from the body to the brain*, giving it **feedback** about what your body is up to.

The bit of the brain that *senses* body movement is called the **sensory** (or if you're really posh, **somatosensory**) **cortex**. Again, it sits on the top edge of the brain, forming a second girl's hairband that lies just behind that of the motor cortex.

Signals travel to the sensory cortex from the muscles, tendons, fascia, skin and other organs and tissues throughout the body, via **sensory neurons**. There's at least one sensory neuron within every muscle and tendon in your body, and some muscles contain hundreds of sensory neurons.

Together, these sensory neurons send millions of sensory signals to the brain every second, giving it **non-stop feedback**. This tells the brain *where each muscle, bone and limb is in space*, what the *angles* are between them, and *how tense or relaxed* each muscle and tendon is.

But how does knowing where your limbs are help you return a super-fast tennis serve?

Ah, but the sensory part of the nervous system also receives signals from the eyes, ears, and other **sensory organs**. By combining these signals, your nervous system allows you to *observe* what's going on and *orient* yourself towards it.

So returning the serve begins with seeing it ('there's a tennis ball flying at me'), then proceeds to taking stock of *where you are* ('I'm facing the ball, feet apart, racquet down'). Next, you have to *decide* what you're going to do ('turn sideways, raise the racquet, prepare to hit the ball'), and *do* it ('turn, lift racquet, hit ball!').

But don't the *deciding* and *doing* parts mean that you have to *think*?

Not necessarily. Train hard enough, and your nervous system will decide and act *for* you. This brings us to the third major job of the nervous system in the body: **interpreting**.

In addition to **moving** and **sensing** things, your nervous system also **interprets** – or makes sense of – *the information* relayed by the sensory neurons, and uses this information to *build new motor skills and movements*. This happens almost entirely within the brain, and uses many different regions of the brain – from the outer **cortex** to the deeper **forebrain**, **midbrain** and **hindbrain**.

By combining the information from motor signals and sensory signals, the brain can 'test out' new, complex muscle movements and learn – by trial and error – how best to accomplish them. This is how you learn precise, sport-related skills and movements, like returning a tennis serve, shooting a football, catching a basketball, or whacking a cricket ball right out of the grounds.

In the beginning, all complex movements like this are difficult, but, with repetition, they eventually become *automatic*, something your body knows how to do without thinking. We call this body-movement autopilot **muscle memory** (we first met this in chapter one, remember?). *This* is what allows a top tennis player to return a 150mph serve.

I could return a serve like that easily. If I wanted to.
No way!

Wanna bet?
Fine. How would you do it?

Easy. You just wait until the ball's gone past at 150mph.
OK...

Then you turn round, pick the ball up, walk over to the net, and hand it to the other player. Bingo — serve returned.
But that's cheating!

Too late! You lose, sucker! Bwahahahahahaa!

'Luck has nothing to do with it, because I have spent many, many hours, countless hours, on the court working for my one moment in time, not knowing when it would come.'

Serena Williams,
former world number-one women's tennis player,
and winner of two Olympic golds in women's doubles

Table Tennis/Ping-Pong

How to play
A two- or four-player game in which players hit a tiny, lightweight ball between two halves of a hard table divided by a low, central net. As in tennis, the ball must land within your opponents' (table) area to remain in play, and if it bounces twice – or your opponent fails to return it after one bounce – you win the point. It's like tennis, only on a table. Get it? But because the 'court' is so much smaller – and the players so much closer together, table tennis is *much* faster.

Players
For singles matches, two players play head-to-head.
For doubles matches, four players battle it out two a side.

Equipment
Ball – a hollow, air-filled, plastic ball just 40mm in diameter.
Racquet – Also known as a **bat** or **paddle**. A small, solid wooden disc with a short handle attached for gripping. The paddle surface is usually covered with a thin layer of rubber for gripping and spinning the ball.
Table – solid wooden surface, on wooden or metal legs, built to a height of 76cm. The playing surface measures 2.7m x 1.5m, and is divided width-wise by a central net 15cm high.

Scoring
Games are scored in single points, the game being won by the first player to reach eleven points (or two points clear, if the score goes to 10–10). Matches are played to the best out of five or seven games, depending on the tournament type.

Football and Rugby

How do you make a football bend in the air?

*'Bending' a football during a corner or free kick is a tricky task indeed. It involves adding **spin** to the ball, which changes the way air moves around it, in-flight. This is easier said than done, and if you want to 'bend it like Beckham', you'll have to put a lot of practice in.*

You spin the ball? Like with your fingers?

No, of course not. In football, you're not allowed to touch the ball with your hands. That is, unless you're the goalie. Or you're playing **rugby football**, **American football**, **Gaelic football** or **Australian rules football**.

Those are all types of *football*? I thought there was only one!

Well, if you live in the USA, then 'football' automatically means 'American football'. If you live in the UK (or pretty much anywhere else in the world) it usually means 'soccer'. But there are other football games too.

What's the difference between them all?

Well, rugby football, as you probably know, is played with an egg-like (or **ovoid**) ball, rather than a round one. Players can **throw**, **catch** *and* **kick** the ball, as they try to move

it past the opposing team's goal line.

At the start of the game, each team is assigned to one half of the pitch, and aims to score at the opposite end. Play begins with one team kicking the ball deep into the other team's half. Thereafter, players try to **run** or **pass** the ball around opposing players to reach the goal area and **ground** the ball (i.e. touch it to the ground).

But here's the tricky bit: although *kicking the ball forward* is allowed, you can only *pass the ball* (with your hands) *sideways* or *backwards*. This means lots of **tactical positioning** and **blocking**, and dramatic runs of players passing the ball sideways down fast-advancing lines of players.

Rugby Football

How to play

A team game played on a large outdoor field. Players throw, catch and kick an ovoid (egg-shaped) ball, attempting to move it in the opposing team's goal area, and score points by grounding it past the goal line. This grounding, called a '**try**', may then be '**converted**' for extra points, by taking a free kick through the tall, H-shaped goalposts at the end of the pitch. The ball must always be passed backwards or sideways between players, never forward.

There are two types of rugby football game: rugby league and rugby union, each with slightly different rules.

Players

For a rugby union game, thirty players in two teams, playing fifteen a side.

For a rugby league game, twenty-six players, playing thirteen a side.

Equipment
Rugby ball – leather or synthetic ball, around 30cm long, with a circumference of about 62cm round their wide middle. The ovoid shape gives it an unpredictable, irregular bounce, making it hard to judge where it will end up if it's dropped or kicked.
Goalposts – H-shaped posts around 5.6m apart, and at least 4m tall, with a horizontal crossbar bridging between them at a height of 3m. No nets.
Boots – studded boots for gripping turf, similar to football boots.
Gumshield – used, as in boxing, to prevent teeth from being damaged or knocked out.
Headgear – thin, padded helmets that protect the skull and ears. In contrast to American football helmets, these are optional in rugby, and often are worn only by the players who form **scrums** (see later).

But you're not allowed to just *grab* the ball off a rival player, right?

Right. The ball can be **intercepted** by catching an airborne pass, or by **tackling** a player holding the ball. Rugby **tackles** involve diving and grabbing the running player around the legs, hips or torso (**neck tackles** are dangerous and illegal), bringing them *and* the ball to the ground.

Once down, the grounded player *must* release the ball, and players from both teams pile on top, trying to **rake** the ball free with their feet. If the ball comes free and is picked up by a running player, play continues. If the ball gets stuck in this pile-up (also known as a '**ruck**'), then a **scrum** is called.

Is that when the players make a big mob, and push on each other?

That's the one. In a scrum, players on each team lock shoulders to form an offensive formation, and push against each other head-to-head. The ball is rolled into the middle of the scrum, and the **scrummers** attempt to push forward and rake the ball out (hopefully, towards a teammate) with their feet. Without protective headgear, a rough scrum can easily lead to cracked heads and torn, swollen earlobes on both sides.*

Footballing First The oldest rugby club in the world, Dublin University Football Club, was founded in 1854. That was three years before the founding of the first ever soccer club, Sheffield FC, and nine years before the first American football club, the Oneida Football Club. So rugby football was the first *official* type of football!

---

* This is why rugby players can often be spotted off the field by looking for their swollen 'cauliflower' ears.

Teams score *five points* each time they ground the ball in the opposing goal area, scoring a **try**. Right after the try, they are given a **free kick** at the goalposts, from a spot distant from the goal line, but parallel to wherever the try was made. Getting the ball between the posts (and over the crossbar) is called a **conversion**, and earns the scoring team *another two points*, giving a maximum of *seven points* per goal. Points can also be scored for **penalty kicks** and **drop-goals**, which are spontaneous kicks taken at the goal during the game. Each of these, if on target, scores *three points*.

Is that it?

Yep. That's pretty much it for rugby. Australian rules (or 'Aussie rules') and Gaelic football are variations on rugby football, with different rules and tactics.

While rugby is played fifteen a side or thirteen a side on a rectangular pitch, Aussie rules football is an eighteen-a-side game played on an *oval* pitch. It came after (and was almost certainly developed from) rugby, and has similar rules and tactics on the field. But the goalposts (and goal scoring) are quite different. There are four upright goalposts (two tall central posts, with two shorter ones outside them) at each end of the field, and players score by kicking the oval ball between them. If it goes between the tall, central posts, you get *six points*. If it goes outside these, but inside the shorter, outer posts, you get **one** point.

Gaelic football, meanwhile, is a fifteen-a-side game played like a *cross between rugby and soccer*. The ball is round (like a soccer ball), and players may kick it with their feet *and* hold and pass the ball with their hands. But since they're *not allowed to run more than four steps* while holding the ball, they have to bounce it on the ground (like basketball players) or **chip** it ahead of themselves with their feet in order to move it forward.

The goalposts and scoring are also a bit different. The rectangular goals at each end look a bit like **soccer** goals – complete with **nets** and **goalkeepers** – but also have tall upright posts extending 7m into the air on each side, like **rugby** goalposts. Players score *one point* for getting the bar over the crossbar (but between the uprights), or *three points* for putting it in the back of the net.

What about American football? Isn't that just like rugby with pads?

Well, yes and no. The rules of American football are many, and can be tricky to understand (or even remember) in full.

The basic idea is similar to rugby – each team is assigned to one half of the pitch, and aims to score at the opposite end. Eventually, the object is to reach the goal area (or **endzone**) and **ground** the ball to score. But, in practice, this distance is usually covered slowly and gradually, as ball-carrying players are **tackled** or **intercepted** long before they make it to the **endzone**.

In short, the attacking team has four attempts (or **downs**) to get the ball ten yards (9m) down the field. If they manage this, then they're given *four more* attempts to go another four yards (3.6m). This continues until the attacking team gets the ball to the endzone, loses possession of the ball or runs out of time.

Is that why the game seems to start and stop so much?

Right. In contrast to rugby, the ball is *not* up for grabs once a player is tackled. Once a player is brought to the ground, play *stops*, and the attacking and defending teams re-form their positions around this new '**down**' position. There are *no scrums* to decide possession, and there's *no scooping or raking* of the ball once it's on the ground.

So instead of direct tackling, the defending team gains possession of the ball by **catching** (or **intercepting**) an airborne pass, by picking up a ball that has been dropped (or fumbled) by an attacking player, or when the attacking team fails to '**make first down**' (i.e. fails to get the ball ten yards down the field from the position of their last 'down', within four attempts).

Whew! Sounds complicated.

It is. Because of these and other rule differences, the game of American football is far more about **gaining territory** than rugby. It has been described as a cross between '**high-speed sumo**' and '**full-contact chess**'!

American Football (Gridiron)

How to play

A team ball game played on a large outdoor field, which is similar to rugby but played with very different rules and tactics. As in rugby, football players throw, catch and kick an ovoid ball, attempting to move it in the opposing team's goal area, and score points by grounding it past the goal line. This grounding, called a '**touchdown**', may then be '**converted**' for extra points, by taking a free kick through tall, Y-shaped goalposts at the end of the pitch. The main difference is that in American football, the ball *can* be passed forward with a long throw, which makes the game more about tactical blocking, passing and catching than it is about running and tackling. That said, unlike rugby players, American football players also wear extensive padding and head protection, which allows for harder, more violent head-to-head tackling.

Players

Twenty-two players in two teams, playing eleven a side.

Equipment

Football – pointy-ended, ovoid, leather ball, around 30cm long, with a circumference of about 56cm round the middle – a little narrower than a standard rugby ball. The pointed ends help it to fly better during long forward passes.

Goalposts – Y-shaped posts much taller than rugby goalposts. The two-pronged uprights are around 5.6m apart, 9m tall, set above a horizontal crossbar 10m off the ground. No nets.

Helmet – hard-shelled helmet similar to a motorcycle helmet, complete with metal grille to protect the face.
Shoulder and chest pads – thick foam-and-plastic pads to protect the shoulders and chest from thudding impacts.
Hip, thigh and knee pads – made of hard plastic, and worn inside the long-legged trousers to protect the joints and muscles of the legs.

So how do they score points?

Teams score *six points* each time they ground the ball in the opposing goal area, scoring a **touchdown**. Right after, they are given a **free kick** at the goalposts, from a spot on the three-yard (2.7m) line parallel to wherever the touchdown was made. Getting the ball between the posts (and over the crossbar) earns the scoring team *another point*.

Alternatively, the team can try to **run** and **pass** the ball into the endzone, scoring a so-called **two-point conversion**. This gives a maximum of *seven points per goal*. Points can also be scored for **penalty kicks** and **field-goals**, which are spontaneous kicks taken at the goal during the game.

The game of American football is played in four fifteen-minute quarters (going to fifteen minutes of extra time if the score is tied at the end). But since the game clock stops between each major '**play**' (i.e. while the ball is downed and players reset their tactical positions, ready for the next downfield movement), the game usually takes *several hours* to complete.

Yikes.

Yep. By comparison, the game most non-Americans call

football – **Association football,** or **soccer** – is far faster and simpler. *One goal* gets you *one point*. You can control the ball with any part of the body *except* your arms and hands (in practice, mostly **feet**, **head** and **chest**). You play for two forty-five-minute halves, and the team with the most points wins.

It's this beautiful simplicity that has helped to make football the *most popular,* and *most watched,* sporting game in the world. Millions of people in the UK, Europe, South America and elsewhere play football, and follow football league games in their own countries. And every four years, *billions* of people tune in to watch the **World Cup** tournament. In a way, football *unifies* the whole world.

So if football is so much simpler, does that mean it's easier to play than those other types of football too?

Not necessarily. All these games require **agility** – the ability to change your direction of movement quickly and suddenly (we'll learn more about that in the next chapter). But each also has its own set of skills. Rugby **forwards** need to be able to make swift and accurate sideways passes at a full run, while American football **quarterbacks** must be able to throw the ball accurately to a running **receiver** over 50m away.

And football **strikers** and **centre-forwards**, of course, have to learn to **spin** and **bend** a ball through the air, sending it around defensive players and into a goal (or on to the head of a waiting teammate).

Hmmmm. I still don't quite get how that works.

What d'you mean?

I mean, why would spinning the ball affect how it moves through the air?

Why *wouldn't* it?

Well, I get that spin makes a ball bounce funny. That makes sense. It hits the ground with a spin, and comes off at a different angle.

OK...

... but if a spinning ball is just flying through the air, it's not actually *touching anything*, is it?

Ah, but it is. It's touching the *air* around it.

It is?

Of course. When a striker puts spin on a ball, by making contact with it a little to one side of the ball, it *carves its way through the air* as it spins. On one side of the ball, the air will be *moving in the same direction* that the ball is spinning. This makes the air flow over this side of the ball more smoothly, decreasing the pressure of the air against that side of the ball.

On the *opposite* side, the surface of the ball will be spinning, as it were, *into* the wind. This creates **drag** and **turbulence** (churning air), and increases the air pressure on that side of the ball.

Since there's now *more pressure on one side of the ball*

than the other, the ball then **drifts** (or **bends**) to one side – towards the side with lower pressure. In effect, this means the path of the ball will bend away from the foot you struck it with. Hit the ball off-centre with the inside of your *right* foot, and it'll bend *right to left*. Hit it with the inside of your *left* foot, and it'll bend *left to right*.

AIR

ROUGH SPIN SMOOTH

BALL

Is that it? That sounds easy!

Well, it takes many, many hours of practice to learn to hit the ball *just right* for a bend. David Beckham still spends *hours* working on his bending shots every week. But if you're willing to put that much time into it there's no

reason why you couldn't learn to do it too. Who knows? In a few years' time, you could be curling in the winning shot at a World Cup final . . .

‘I still look at myself and want to improve.’

David Beckham,
football legend and former
captain of the England football team

Give it a go!

Exercise: bend it like Beckham
Type: skill
Goal: improve soccer skill

(These instructions are for right-footed players. If you're left-footed, reverse everything!)

1. To curve the ball from *right to left*, use the *inside* of your right foot, striking the *bottom half* of the *right side* of the ball.
2. To curve the ball from *left to right*, use the *outside* of your right foot, striking the *bottom half* of the *left side* of the ball.
3. In both cases, your follow-through will *not* be in the direction of the target goal or player. Instead, imagine you are cutting across the back of the ball rather than kicking through the centre of it.
4. Practise until brilliant. Earn spot on England team. Score a ridiculous number of goals from corners and free kicks. Reclaim glory by winning first World Cup for England since 1966.

Football (Soccer)

How to play

A team ball game, typically* played on a large outdoor pitch. Players kick a large, air-filled, leather or synthetic leather ball – running, dribbling, passing, tackling and scoring points by shooting it into netted goals at each end of the pitch. Statistically, football is the most popular sport in the world.

Players

For the standard game, twenty-two players in two teams of eleven. Ten outfielders plus one goalkeeper on each. Indoor football has ten players, playing five a side.

Equipment

Ball – 70cm in circumference (a little smaller than a basketball), made of heavy leather or synthetic leather. Inside is an air-filled bladder with a polyester/cotton lining, which helps to add bounce.

Goals – tall, wide, netted frames measuring 7.3m x 2.4m.

Boots – studded leather boots that give extra grip on the grassy pitch. Some have special gripping surfaces on the instep to help curl and control the ball.

Shinpads – rubber/plastic shields worn inside long socks to protect delicate shin bones while tackling.

Gloves – worn by the goalkeepers only, for grip and protection of the fingers.

---

* Although other forms of football also exist. Indoor football (also known as 'futsal' or 'five-a-side' is played on a smaller indoor court with walls, while beach soccer is played – you guessed it – on a sandy beach.

Cricket, Baseball and Softball

Which is harder to hit, a baseball or a cricket ball?

*That all depends on who's throwing it, and how. In general, baseballs are **pitched** faster than cricket balls are **bowled**. But when a spinning cricket ball is bounced, it can behave in much crazier ways.*

How fast do baseballs go, compared to cricket balls?

Actually, the top speed reached by a thrown cricket ball or baseball is roughly the same. Top cricket **fast-bowlers** can deliver looping, straight-armed throws that release the ball at over 100mph (160km/h). Top baseball pitchers, meanwhile, deliver fastball throws at around 105mph (168km/h) – just 5mph faster. That said, baseball pitchers deliver the balls at over 90mph much more often.

Why's that?

Mostly because they are allowed to throw the ball with a *bent elbow*. In cricket, this is not permitted, as bowlers have to keep their arms straight and within fifteen degrees of vertical as they release the ball. So, in general, baseball players at the bat face a faster ball than cricket players.

The different shape of the bats used in each sport also makes a big difference. The **blade** of a **cricket bat** is flat, offering more surface area for the ball to make contact with. The **barrel** of a **baseball bat**, meanwhile, is a tapering **cylinder**. Its narrow, rounded striking surface is much harder to place against the ball in mid-swing.

Cricket

How to play
A team game played on a large, oval, outdoor field, centred on a small, oblong **pitch**. One team's thrower (or **bowler**) lobs a small, hard ball towards one of three knee-height wooden targets called a **wicket**. The other team's **batsman** attempts to defend the wicket, hit the ball and score points by running back and forth between the two wickets as many times as possible (making **runs**) before the ball is returned by catchers (or **fielders**) spread throughout the field.

Players
Twenty-two– two teams, playing eleven a side.

Equipment
Cricket ball – 23cm in circumference, made of cork, wound string and (natural or synthetic) leather. About the same size as a tennis ball, but, being solid rather than air-filled, it's *far* heavier and harder.
Cricket bat – a flat wooden blade, traditionally made of willow, with a gripped handle. Just under 1m in length.
Gloves, helmet (with facemask), leg pads, box – worn by batsmen and **wicket-keepers** (catchers) only. Helps prevent breaks, bruises and other injuries.*

---

* A fast-bowled cricket ball to the head or chest can be lethal, and without shin pads you can almost guarantee bruised or cracked shin bones. After all, as a batsman, you're essentially standing in front of the target. So you can't blame the bowler for aiming your way . . .

Scoring

The batsman tries to intercept the ball and hit it towards the oval boundary line marking the edge of the field. If the ball rolls across this, he scores *four runs*. If the ball flies over this, he scores *six runs*. Otherwise, the batsmen try to run as many times as possible between the wickets before the fielders return the ball (typically scoring just one or two runs per hit). The bowler stays at the same wicket, and bowls towards whichever batsman has arrived at the opposite wicket during the previous hit-and-run.

Play continues like this until a batsman goes out (see below), or the bowler has delivered six on-target throws, which is called an **over**. At this point, the **umpire** (referee) calls 'over', and the new bowler switches ends – now bowling from behind the opposite wicket.

If the wickets are hit by the ball, the batsman is **bowled out**, and another batsman from the same team takes his place. Likewise, if a batsman hits the ball into the air, and a fielder catches it, the batsman is **caught out**. And if a batsman fails to make it to one of the wickets before the fielders return the ball and knock off the bails, then he is **run out**.

Play continues until the end of an **innings**. At this point, the batting and fielding teams switch roles. The innings comes to an end in one of three ways:

1. Ten of the eleven members of a batting team are **bowled**, **caught** or **run out**.
2. The bowler has bowled a certain **number of overs** (sets of six on-target throws). The number of overs per innings varies from twenty overs (or 120 throws) in 20/20 and beach cricket to more than fifty overs (or 200 throws) in longer matches.

3. The allocated time for an innings is up. Again, this varies from seventy-five minutes or less (in 20/20 cricket or beach cricket) to an entire day. Test matches have no time limits on innings at all (which is one reason why they take several days to play).

Teams score points only when their batsmen score runs. So the object of the game is to (a) *score as many runs as possible while batting*, and (b) *get the opposing batsmen out as soon as possible when fielding*, so that they cannot score so many runs.

This is what leads to the tension and excitement of multi-day cricket – when the scores are close and only a few batsmen left 'in', the pressure is on to get these last few out before they can draw level or overtake the team who batted last.

In many ways, cricket is like multi-day 'endurance baseball', played in a straight line. Or, looked at another way, baseball is a bit like fast-paced, circular cricket.

There you go, then. That means baseballs are harder to hit, right?

Well, not necessarily. As that's not quite the end of the story . . .

You see, unlike baseballs, cricket balls may **bounce** before they reach the batsman. This changes the flightpath of the ball a lot when the ball is thrown with a **spin**.

In cricket, spin bowlers are perhaps the most feared players in the game. Spin bowlers purposely add **topspin**, **backspin** or **sidespin** to the ball by flicking the wrist and fingers as they release the ball. When the ball bounces, this affects the frictional forces between the ball and the ground, altering its path towards the batsman.

Like how?

A ball thrown with no extra spin will **approach** and **rebound** off the ground at *more or less the same angle*. It's like placing a mirror at the spot where the ball bounces – the **approach line** of the ball on one side mirrors the **exit line** on the other. The batsman anticipates this, and prepares to hit the ball based on this even bounce-angle.

But if the ball is spinning when it contacts the ground the angle of the exit line changes. **Topspin** *reinforces the forward spin* added to the ball by **friction** as it bounces. This makes the ball exit the bounce at a *lower angle* than expected. **Backspin** partly *cancels out the forward spin*

WITHOUT SPIN

WITH SPIN

added by friction, which makes the ball bounce upward, at a *higher angle* than expected. And adding spin to the left or right side of the ball (cricketers call this **offspin** and **legspin**) creates **lateral friction** between the ball and the ground, making the ball zigzag to the left or right after the bounce.

Put this together, and you can see that bowlers can create a variety of awkward and unpredictable angles with a quick flick of the wrist. Most non-professional batsmen could never hope to hit a ball bowled this way.

Tricky, tricky. So why don't baseball pitchers bounce the ball?

In short, because they're not *allowed* to. Plus baseballs don't bounce as much, and the pitches are made across an earth-covered diamond of ground, rather than the close-cropped grass of a cricket pitch. So the ball would lose too much speed on the bounce.

So it's all about throwing as fast as possible, then?

That's one tactic, yes. A 90–100mph fastball travels so fast that the batter can hardly see it. The ball closes on the batter so rapidly that his eyes cannot refocus quickly enough to keep it in clear view. In fact, for the last 3m of its flight, a fastball is practically *invisible* to the batter. All he sees is a white blur.

It's like using a camera with an autofocus device – as you point the camera at something new, it takes time for the lenses to whirr back and forth and focus on the thing at which you're pointing them. Your eyes 'autofocus' too, and generally do it much faster than mechanical cameras. But it still takes time, and if an object is moving fast enough – especially *towards* the viewer – it will become a mere blur as it draws close.

How do batters hit fastballs *at all*, then?

Basically, the batter has to aim *ahead* of the ball, and swing where he *thinks* it's going to go. This means the batter has to commit to his swing when ball is still over 6m away. If the ball travels in a straight line from this point, then the batter has a good chance of hitting it, as he can predict where it's likely to end up.

The trouble is that the pitcher has another trick up his sleeve – another tactic besides 'throw really fast'.

What's that?

He (or she) can make the ball **curve**, **dip** or **swerve** off that straight path, tricking the batter into predicting (and swinging at) a path that the ball will not take. Where cricket bowlers alter the path of the ball *on the bounce*, baseball pitchers have developed a wide range of **dipping**, **curving** and **swerving** throws to alter the path of the ball *in mid-air*.

How do they do that?

They do it using the same principle as the ball-bending football strikers we met in the last section. Add spin to *one side* of the ball, and uneven airflow across its surface will make it swerve towards the *opposite side*. So, while **fastballs** are thrown hard and straight, adding topspin, backspin or sidespin to the throw produces slower, looping **sliders**, **screwballs** and **curveballs**.

Baseball

How to play

A team game played on a large outdoor field, centred on a small, square 'diamond' with a 'base' at each corner. One team's thrower (or **pitcher**) stands on an earth **mound** in the centre of the diamond, while the opposing team's batter stands at the **home plate**, the first of the diamond's four corners. The pitcher throws a small, hard ball towards a **catcher*** crouching behind the batter at the home plate. The batter attempts to hit the ball (preferably right out of the stadium) and scores points by running round the four corners of the diamond, covering as many '**bases**' as possible before the ball is returned by fielders. If the batter makes it all the way round in one go, it's called a **home run**.** Points are scored for every batter who makes it back to home base.

Players

Eighteen – two teams, nine per side.

Equipment

Baseball – 7.5cm in diameter, made of cork, rubber, cotton and leather. Although not quite as hard as a cricket ball, these are still no joke if they hit you in the head.

Baseball bat – solid cylinder of wood or metal, thicker at the hitting end (or barrel), and thinner towards the gripping end. A wide knob at the end of the bat grip prevents the bat slipping from the batter's hands.

---

* In contrast to the wicket-keeper in cricket, the baseball catcher communicates with the pitcher, suggesting types and angles of throw. The two teammates work together to try to get the ball past the batter and into the catcher's hands. They even have special finger signals for each type of throw.

** While this sometimes happens, more often they only make it to one or two bases before they have to stop. But they can run on after the next batter hits the ball, or even 'steal' bases by running between them while the pitcher isn't looking. So while cricket is all about fair play, in baseball, 'sneaky' is the way forward.

Helmet – worn by batters, for head protection.

Mitt – a single wide leather glove worn by pitchers and fielders. This is worn on the non-throwing hand to assist with catching.

Mask, chest protector, knee pads, shin pads – worn by the catcher only, to protect against fast ball impacts.

Scoring

As in cricket, play begins with deciding who gets to bat or field first. Traditionally, the visiting team bats first – sending a single batter to the home plate – while the other sends a pitcher to the mound, a catcher to the home plate, and positions its fielders throughout the field.

The pitcher then throws the ball overarm towards the catcher's mitt, using one of several pitch types to try to outfox the batter. The batter then tries to intercept the ball, hit it towards the edge of the field and run round as many bases as possible before the fielders return the ball. Whether he makes it all the way round, or just to one or two bases, another batter then steps up to the plate and takes his turn to bat.

If the ball is hit, but the fielders get it to the first base before the batter can run there, this is called a **ground out**. As in cricket, a batter is also **caught out** if he hits the ball into the air, and a fielder catches it. In either case, it's not just the batter that leaves the field – any remaining batters waiting at the other three bases must go too. Batters can also be **tagged out** by a fielder touching them with the ball while they run between bases.

Play continues this way until three **outs** are made, at which point the 'top' half of the inning ends. In the second (or 'bottom') half, the teams switch roles – the batting team takes to the field, and the pitching/fielding team goes to bat. When three more outs are made, the inning ends.*

As in cricket, points are scored only for **runs** (not outs), and the object of the game is to score runs while preventing the other team from doing so (by getting their batters **out** as quickly as possible). If one team has a clear lead after nine innings, the game ends. If they are still drawn at this point, then extra innings are played until one team leads at the end of an inning.**

Like cricket, baseball is something of an endurance game, played over many hours. But with more ways to score runs – and shorter, faster-paced innings – it can be more fun for those who like their games to last *less* than an entire day.

Sliders and screwballs bend to the right or left, just like Beckham's soccer shots. Curveballs, meanwhile, dip downward as they approach the batter. And that's just for starters. Other pitch types include the **cutter**, **splitter** and **changeup**. Each one has its own spin and throwing angle, and its own, special flightpath. There's even one called a **slurve**, which is a cross between a **slider** and a **curveball**.

Blimey. I have trouble throwing a ball straight, let alone making it curve and dip. How do they learn to throw like that?

The same way archers learn to shoot bows, basketballers learn to shoot baskets and tennis players learn to serve

---

* So a full inning sees each team getting a chance to bat once, and going 'out' three times.

** Remember, baseball innings have two halves, giving both teams a chance to bat and score, so this 'drawing level' process can continue for a while. The longest big-league game ever played went to twenty-five innings, and lasted almost nine hours!

and return tennis balls at breakneck speeds. They do it by training their nervous systems, and by creating what scientists call **muscle memory**.

Here's how it works. When you first practise any new movement skill, you have to concentrate hard, and large areas of your brain are involved.

Imagine holding a cricket ball (or baseball) for the first time, and trying to throw it past a batsman, and straight towards a wicket (or catcher). The first few times you do it, you'll be lucky if you get the ball anywhere near on target. The ball will probably drop short of the batsman, fly over his head or fly off to one side. At this point, your eyes, muscles, nerves and brain are working furiously just to coordinate throwing the ball correctly. This is the first level of learning – the level of **deliberate action**.

OK. Then what?

Later, you get the hang of throwing the ball, and you can actually hit the wicket (or pitch it into the catcher's glove) at least nine times out of ten. It's travelling *straight* and *slow*, so it's not going to get past a decent batsman yet, but at least it's going somewhere. This means your brain has learned how to angle your arm to deliver the ball straight, but you can't yet control how hard you throw it *and* which direction the ball will go at the same time. You either throw *hard and miss*, or *throw softly and get it on target*.

That pretty much describes where I'm at now.

OK, that's fine. Now with *even more* practice, your brain will continue to interpret signals from your muscles and eyes, allowing you to make small corrections to the angle of your hand, wrist, shoulder and elbow.

Eventually, you (or rather your brain) will figure out the right combination of muscle movements, and with effort and concentration, you'll start throwing the ball **hard**, **fast** *and* **on target**. Later on, your brain will group all this muscle movement data together, and file it deeper within your brain, largely in a region of your hindbrain call the **cerebellum**.

Congratulations – you have now successfully created a **muscle memory** for bowling or pitching a ball, and you'll probably never forget how this basic action is performed. You can now throw a ball fast towards a wicket or catcher pretty much *automatically*.

This is pretty much how *all* new complex motor skills are learned. And it explains why you can't just serve a tennis ball, chip a football or throw a fastball on your first try. It takes **time** and **practice** for your brain to *figure out* how to do it. And even more time and practice for it to *remember* how to do it.

But how do you go from that to spin-bowling and screwballs?

Well, even when a complex movement like throwing a ball becomes automatic, that's still not the end of the story. It takes *yet more practice* to *perfect* the movement, and turn it into something you can *use* in a variety of sporty situations.

The more you practise, the more corrections are made to the basic, automatic movement you have already learned, and the better you get at doing it. Before long, you'll have created a whole set of new muscle memories, and you'll be spin-bowling and slurving with the best of them.

Niiiice. So how long does it take to become an expert bowler or pitcher?

The old saying just happens to be right – as far as super-powered sports skills are concerned – *practice makes perfect*.

It takes just *5–10 hours* of practice to learn how to kick or throw a ball reliably. Most of us accomplish that in a couple of afternoons' worth of play as a small child.

But, as we've already learned, many experts reckon it takes 5,000–10,000 hours to perfect any skill like this, whether it's fast-bowling at 100mph, pitching a perfect curveball, or blasting a football from outside the penalty area, curling it round a diving goalkeeper and burying it in the top corner of the net.

All right, but let's say I got so good at pitching baseballs that I invented my own type of throw. Could I name it?

I suppose so.

Cool. In that case, I'm going to create a cross between a splitter and a cutter.

What will you call it?

A splutter!

Good luck with that . . .

Give it a go!

Exercise 1: bowl a crafty leg spin
Type: skill
Goal: improve cricket skills, dexterity

1. Place the cricket ball in your hand with the top joints of the index and middle fingers across the seam, with the ball resting between a bent third finger and the thumb. Your bent little finger braces against the ball from beneath.
2. Take your run-up and bowl the ball overarm towards the batsman's leg side (his right, if he's right-handed).
3. As you release the ball, straighten the fingers and allow it to spin off your ring finger, turning the ball anti-clockwise.
4. Flick the wrist so that the palm of the hand finishes facing downward.
5. As the ball bounces, the spin should cause it to turn to the batsman's off (batting) side – so he expects it to go one way, but it bounces the other.
6. Aim just to the right of the batsman, and you can bounce it back towards the wicket, laughing and cheering as he takes a useless swipe at where he *thought* it would go, and watches helplessly as it hits the stumps. *Howzat?!*

Exercise 2: pitch a wicked curveball
Type: skill
Goal: improve baseball skills, dexterity

1. Grip the baseball with your middle and index fingers together, with the fingers across the seams of the ball at the widest part (the widest distance between the seams).
2. Keep a tight grip on the ball, especially with the middle finger.
3. Don't let the ball touch the palm of your hand, or you won't generate enough topspin, which is what allows the ball to drop when it gets close to the batter.
4. Throw an overarm pitch, but make sure your hand and forearm travel top to bottom, like you're chopping something with an axe.
5. When throwing, keep your wrist cocked and turned towards your body – the ball and the palm of your hand should be facing toward you.
6. Keep your elbow up, turn your wrist and *snap* your wrist down as you release the ball. This snap is essential, or the ball will not dip.
7. Watch and laugh as the batter swings high, and the ball dips low. STRIKE ONE! Two more, and he's out of there . . .

Softball and Rounders

How to play

These are team games, similar to baseball, usually played on a slightly smaller field. Both are older forerunners of the harder, faster game of baseball. As in baseball, one team's pitcher or bowler throws towards an opposing batter, and the batter tries to hit the ball and score points by running round four bases arranged into a diamond. But both softball and rounders use a larger, softer* ball, which is thrown underarm, rather than overarm. This makes the ball easier to hit, and the game easier to play.

Players

In softball, eighteen to twenty – two teams of nine or ten.

In rounders, anything from ten to thirty players, with five to fifteen** on each team.

Equipment

Ball – a softball is 30.5cm in circumference, and much less dense than a baseball. A rounders ball is smaller – about 20cm in circumference – but a little harder. Both are made of cork, rubber and leather.

Bat – shorter than baseball bats. Made of wood or aluminium. Softball and rounders bats can be no longer than 86cm. Rounders bats are often half this size, and used one-handed by batters.

Helmet, glove – used in softball, but not rounders.

---

* Hence the name 'softball', geddit? On the flipside, baseball is also known as 'hardball'.

** Both teams must have the same number, obviously. It'd hardly be fair to have five fielders on one team and fourteen on the other, would it?

Scoring

The rules of softball are very much like those of baseball. Players score **runs** and are **struck**, **caught** and **tagged out** in much the same way. But most softball games only go to five or seven innings, compared with nine in baseball. It's basically a slightly tamer version of baseball.

Rounders is similar to softball in general play, but different in that the flat bases are replaced by 1.2m vertical posts, and batters are **run out** when the fielder touches the ball to these posts, rather than the players themselves. Also, batters can score **half-runs** (or **half-rounders**) by reaching the second or third post after a hit, and the inning ends when *all* batters are called out (rather than the three 'outs' required in baseball).

Finally, when a single batter remains, he/she may continue batting indefinitely as long as they can keep scoring whole **rounders** (equivalent to home runs) that bring them back to the home base. This can make for a very exciting game finale!

Hockey, Hurling, Shinty and Lacrosse

How do hockey players avoid hurting each other?

In **field hockey**, they wear pads on their shins and avoid swinging the stick too high. In **ice hockey**, they wear lots of body armour and slam into each other to their heart's content. And in **hurling**, **shinty** and **lacrosse**, they swing their sticks high, but do their best not to hit each other too hard. Most of the time, they succeed . . .

Most of the time?

Err . . . yes. While players of all these sports try to play safely, some – ahem – try a bit harder than others. So you do get the occasional broken leg. Or rib. Or skull.

Yikes! I thought hockey was a safe game.

Well, for the most part, **field hockey** is safe. The other hockey variants, a little less so.

In field hockey, every player wields a **hockey stick**. But when they swing it they're aiming for the ball, not each other. Players use their sticks to:

Push – scoot the ball along the ground
Flick – scoop the ball into the air
Drive – swing at the ball like a golfer, for hard shots
Dribble – run, keeping the ball in front of them with deft taps to either side.

The players use these manoeuvres to go around (not *through*) each other. In this way, field hockey is played a lot like football. But, rather than foot control, hockey is all about **stick control** – players cannot kick the ball, or control it with any other part of their body.*

To keep everyone safe, there are also lots of rules against dangerous play. Players are not allowed to hit (or **volley**) the ball while it's in the air, nor are they allowed to *raise their sticks above shoulder level* to control a high ball. Nor are they allowed to *hit each other* with the sticks.

---

* The only exception to this is the **goalkeeper**, who is allowed to kick the ball and deflect it with any part of the body. In fact, goalies wear special armoured toecaps called **kickers**, specifically for this purpose.

Field Hockey

How to play
A team game played on a large outdoor field. Players pass, dribble and shoot a small, hard ball using long, crook-like wooden sticks. Points are scored by shooting the ball into netted goals found at each end of the field, protected by armoured goalkeepers.

Players
Twenty-two – two teams playing eleven a side, with one goalkeeper on each team.

Equipment
Hockey ball – approximately 8cm in diameter, made of cork and plastic, or just solid plastic. Small and hard, with very little bounce.

Hockey stick – J-shaped wooden stick around 90cm long, with a tubular handle for gripping and a flat, hooked end for striking the ball.

Shin guards – plastic shields worn under long socks to protect the shin bones from bruising and breaks.

Helmet, body protector, leg pads – foam and plastic pads worn by the goalkeeper only, to protect against rocketing hockey-ball impacts.

Scoring
Teams score points by shooting the ball into the goals. But shots taken from outside the shooting circle – a 15m semicircle around each goal – are disallowed and not counted. Successful goals score one point each, and the team with the most goals at the end wins. The game is played in two 35-minute halves.

But how do they avoid hitting each other? I mean, with all those players and sticks on the field, someone's going to get hit sometime. Even if it's only by accident.

That's true. Unlike individual athletic and endurance sports, team ball sports like hockey are also chaotic. Throwing a javelin or doing a pole vault is difficult, certainly. But with nobody running at you while you do it, you can at least take your time and get it right.

In **team sports**, you rarely have the luxury of lining up the perfect throw or shot. With so many players moving around on the field at once, it's hard to predict, moment by moment, where everyone on the field will end up, where you'll have to shoot from, and how much time you'll have to take the shot. Shoot too soon or too late, and you could miss entirely. Or, worse yet, hurt somebody.

Because of this, team games require an extra-special sporting ability – **dexterity**. Dexterity is the ability to *adapt your movements quickly* to any given situation, or use your motor skills to solve problems. This is how hockey players get around each other on the field, and avoid hitting each other when they don't want to.

So other athletes don't need dexterity?

They do, yes. Just not as much. Let me explain . . .

Running in a straight line or throwing a javelin requires strength, skill and power. But they don't require you to adapt your movements to your surroundings, or to a fast-changing situation. Now, if you were being chased by a pack of hungry wolves, or you had to throw that javelin at a sprinting, dodging rabbit, *that* would require dexterity.

In team ball sports, a **high level of dexterity** is needed for **dodging**, **chasing**, **angling** and **adapting** to the movements of opponents. As such, ball sports like **football**, **tennis** and **basketball**, require a lot of dexterity, as each player has to adapt to the fast, crazy, chaotic movements of a flying, bouncing ball.

What's more, many ball sports are also played in **teams** competing head-to-head. This, too, requires dexterity, and *every player* on the team has to adapt to the movements of *every other player* on his own team, *plus all those on the opposing team*. That's a lot of thinking and moving to do on the fly!

So how do we do it?

In the body and brain, dexterity usually develops hand-in-hand with **balance** and **agility.** First, you learn to control your own movements, then you learn how to quickly change the direction of those movements and adapt them to those of your environment.

We'll be learning more about balance, agility *and* dexterity work in the next chapter. But if you want to see your dexterity in action right now, grab a few friends and try this exercise.

Give it a go!

Exercise: flocking
Type: skill
Goal: increase agility and dexterity on the move

1. Grab three or more friends. The more, the better.

2. Start by standing in a wide circle – roughly 5–6m apart – with everybody facing into the centre.
3. Slowly at first, everybody begins walking forward in a straight line. As you approach other walkers, try to move around them without altering your path too much (i.e. keep the straightest line possible without bumping into anyone).
4. Once you've gone 5–6m, turn round and walk back the way you came. Choose a slightly different path (or line) back across the imaginary circle. Again, stick to your line as best you can without hitting anyone.
5. Speed up to a brisk walking pace. Continue dodging around each other.
6. Now speed up to a light jog. Again, keep dodging and moving. Notice how this becomes easier if you relax, breathe and keep your eyes from focusing on any one person. Try to take in the whole group with your vision, and your brain will eventually learn to adjust and predict the paths of everybody in the group, allowing you to flock around them like a bird! This task requires a high degree of agility and dexterity to accomplish. Practice makes perfect!

Not so easy is it? Even walking around each other can be tricky at first. Now imagine doing that on the run, while passing and shooting a ball with a stick – as they do in field hockey.

Think about how much *more* dexterity you'd need for an **ice hockey** game, where you'd have to do the whole thing on ice skates!

Ice Hockey

How to play

A team game typically played on a large indoor ice rink. Players on ice skates whizz about the ice, pushing, dribbling and smashing a small, flat disk (or **puck**) with long sticks ending in a flat, angled blade. Points are scored by shooting the puck into netted goals found at each end of the playing area, guarded by armoured goalkeepers. It's full-contact hockey on ice, but with enough differences to make it a unique and exciting game.

Players

Twelve – two teams playing six a side, including one goalie on each team.

Equipment

Puck – disc 7.5cm in diameter and 2.5cm thick, made of heavy vulcanized rubber or plastic. Hockey pucks rocket across the ice at speeds of over 100mph (160km/h), which is one reason why the goalies are so heavily armoured.

Stick – at 2m, ice hockey sticks are over twice as long as those used in field hockey. But, unlike field hockey sticks, they are reinforced with fibreglass, and the flat blade is angled at 45° to the handle, allowing the base of the blade to lie flat on the ice.

Skates – leather boots with a steel toecap and steel skating blades. Lined with cotton and other materials for warmth.

Helmet – a hard plastic helmet with a cage-like steel face guard. Essential to prevent stray sticks and pucks from cracking into eyes and cheekbones. Goalie helmets have a thicker, stronger face guard, more like a knight's visor.

Shoulder pads and chest guard – protect against impacts from sticks, pucks, other players and nasty falls on the hard, unforgiving ice.

Puck-proof vest and trousers – extra protective clothing worn only by the goalie, lined with tough steel mesh to protect against rocketing puck shots.

Scoring

Teams score points by shooting the puck into the goals, with all goals earning one point, regardless of where on the ice they were shot from. When fouls are committed, play is stopped, then restarted with a face-off at the closest one of five circles and nine spots positioned around the ice.

The game time runs to an hour, played in three twenty-minute periods. But, since the clock stops when play stops, playing a full game can take up to twice as long.

How on earth do hockey players dodge and weave like that on ice skates? I mean, wouldn't they just slip over if they tried to turn too quickly?

Well, ice skates slide around on top of the ice because they focus all your weight into a pair of thin, metal blades beneath your feet. This creates enormous pressure over a small surface area of the ice, causing it to melt into thin strips of water beneath each blade. Provided that you keep the skates level, you can glide forward or backwards on this thin layer of 'instant water' with very little **friction** to slow you down.

When they want to **turn** or **stop**, hockey players (and indeed all ice-skaters) dig the *edges* of their blades into the ice, creating ridges in the ice that push back against the skate – **increasing friction** and *slowing* or *altering* their movements.

Starting and stopping *quickly* can be tough, so falls and collisions do happen in ice hockey. But in general, ice-hockey players are very skilled skaters, and move much faster about the playing area than their counterparts in grass-based **field hockey.**

Is that pretty much all ice hockey is, then? Fast field-hockey-on-ice?

Actually, it's far more than that. For starters, the **ice rink** it's played on is surrounded by a wall of 1m wooden boards.* In field hockey, any ball hit off the field stops play, and the opposing team gets a **push-in** (like a **throw-in**, in football). But, in ice hockey, the players can bounce the puck off the bordering walls, ricocheting it around their opponents.

They can also move *past* and *behind* the goals, and are allowed to control the puck with their feet (skates) or bodies. None of this is allowed in field hockey.

Perhaps most importantly, ice hockey is a **full-contact** game. In field hockey, body contact will earn you a foul, but in ice hockey, players are allowed to **body-check** (i.e. barge into) each other, slamming each other off their feet and even into the plexiglas walls around the rink.

Ouch!

And although it *is* supposed to be illegal to hit opponents with elbows, knees and parts of your stick, this *can* and *does* happen. **Illegal tackles** like this earn **fouls** and get

---

* This wooden wall is topped by a taller transparent one made of plexiglas, to protect the spectators from high-flying pucks.

the player temporarily sent off, leaving their team short of players on the ice. During this time, players have to skate off the ice and into a **penalty box**, staying there for two minutes (for a minor penalty) or five minutes (for a major one).

'I wasn't naturally gifted in terms of size and speed; everything I did in hockey I worked for.'

Wayne Gretzky,
champion ice-hockey player and three-times gold-medal winner in the Canada Cup championships

So while dangerous play gets players permanently sent off in field hockey and soccer, in ice hockey, it just earns you a temporary **'time-out'**! As you might imagine, this makes the game *quite a bit rougher* – hence the need for the extra padding and protection worn by the players.

Pads are also worn to protect players in the hockey-like game of **lacrosse**. Lacrosse is played on outdoor fields, using specially made sticks (a stick is called a **cross**) with a netted pocket at one end.

What do they do with that?

The cross is used to **scoop** the ball from the ground, to

catch the ball in mid-air and
to **pass** or **shoot** the ball with fast
whipping motions – done standing still or at
a full run. Long passes and fast shots are made by whipping
the cross forward from behind the head or shoulders. This
makes the ball travel incredibly fast. Shots and passes
commonly hit breathtaking (and, frankly, dangerous)
speeds of 120mph (200km/h) or more.

Lacrosse

How to play

A team game played on a large outdoor field. Players throw,
catch, scoop, pass and shoot a hard rubber ball using long
sticks with netted pockets at one end. Points are scored by
shooting the ball into netted hoops found at each end of
the field. Lacrosse is like a fast, furious, airborne version of
field hockey, and is not for the faint of heart!

Players

For men's lacrosse – twenty players, in two teams of ten.

For women's lacrosse – twenty-four players, in two
teams of twelve.

Equipment

Ball – 6.5cm in diameter, made of heavy rubber with a lead centre. A little smaller and softer than a field hockey ball, but not much.

Cross – lacrosse sticks (or **crosses**), come in two main sizes. Defenders and goalies use long 1.8m crosses for long throws, while attackers and midfielders use shorter 1m crosses that are easier to move and shoot with. Both types feature a long, tubular handle ending with a wide, netted pocket for catching, carrying and flinging the ball.

Helmet – hard plastic helmet with metal face guard, worn by all players to protect against high-speed, high-flying ball impacts, along with the occasional stick in the face. In women's lacrosse, players wear goggles instead. In the men's game, players also wear protective shoulder and elbow pads and gloves.

Scoring

Teams score points by shooting the ball into the goal, and all shots score one point, regardless of where they are launched from.

Men's lacrosse is played in four quarters of fifteen minutes each. Women's lacrosse games are played in two halves of thirty minutes each. The game can also be played in timed quarters lasting eight or twelve minutes, for younger and more inexperienced players. So the full game lasts anywhere from thirty-two minutes to an hour.

Cool! And they're allowed to *run* with the ball in their stick-pockets too?

Yep. Running with the ball is pretty simple in lacrosse compared with other ball sports. In basketball you have to **bounce** the ball as you run; in soccer and hockey, you have to **dribble** the ball by knocking it ahead of you; in handball and netball, you **can't run** with the ball at all. In lacrosse, you simply **scoop** or **catch the ball in the net** of your stick (or **cross**), and **run with it**.

That sounds a lot easier than hockey.

Ah, but here's the flipside: lacrosse, like ice hockey, is also a **contact sport**. And, just as in ice hockey, **body-checking** and **barging** into players is permitted – as long as it's done from the front or side. Plus the rules require that the defensive players must stay in the defending (rear) half of the field, while attackers must stay in the attacking, forward half. Only the midfielders can roam freely. So in practice, most players don't run far before they're **blocked** or **forced to pass**.

With all the sticks and balls flying about the place, headgear and padding is essential to avoid injury in lacrosse. But, for the most part, the players make efforts not to swing their sticks at each other. The same can't necessarily be said for the even rougher hockey-like games of **hurling** and **shinty** – popular in Ireland and Scotland, respectively.

How are they different, then?

Well, both games use sticks and balls, and shooting happens much as it does in field hockey, with the added bonus that players are allowed to **strike** (or **volley**) the ball while it's still in the air. Shinty and hurling players, though, rarely wear protective padding, and **passing**, **dribbling** and **tackling** can be quite different.

In **hurling**, players dribble by bouncing the ball on the flat blade of the hurley stick – turning the stick on its side and holding it before them as they run. They may also **catch**, **kick** and **throw** the ball, but are *not* allowed to pick the ball up from the ground with their hands, nor pass it from hand to hand. **Tackles** can be made using the **hurley stick**, but should always be directed at the ball, rather than the player. *Most* of the time, they are.

Shinty dribbling looks similar to that of field hockey, except that both sides of the flat **caman stick** can be used to tip-tap the ball on each side.* But passes can be **flipped up** and **smacked** through the air, and shinty players are allowed to use their sticks to **block** and **tackle** other players. At times, this can make shinty look more like a medieval stick-fight than a ball game!

---

* In hockey, players can only use the flat side, so have to keep flipping the blade over as they dribble the ball. In hurling, they can use either side of the stick.

And they don't wear any pads or helmets?

Helmets, yes. Padding, no. They're a tough bunch, those Celts. In fact, ancient Celtic tribes and clans are thought to have played games like hurling and shinty to prepare for real-life battles! Some sports will make you brave, but hurling and shinty will leave you fearless!

. . . or unconscious.

That too.

Give it a go!

Exercise: flocking/passing drill
Type: skill
Goal: increase agility and dexterity on the move

1. Grab three or more friends, a hockey stick each and a hockey or tennis ball.
2. Start the 'flocking' drill in the same way as you did earlier – stand in a wide circle with everybody facing into the centre, then begin walking in straight lines across the circle without bumping into anyone.
3. Now grab your sticks, widen the circle and lower the sticks to the ground as you walk. Before you set off, toss the ball into the centre of the pack of flocking players.
4. Try to contact the ball and pass it to someone else as you move. Walk very slowly at first, but don't stop moving, and don't bump into anyone.
5. Make the circle wider, and speed up your walking pace. Keep passing, keep dodging.
6. Make the circle wider still, and jog or run as you pass the ball and dodge the other players.

This drill is very difficult, as it requires you to concentrate on the movements of the ball *and* the other players. But if you get good at it you'll be a whizz at dribbling and passing around defenders! You can also try a similar drill with a soccer ball or rugby ball – kicking or tossing the ball between the players instead. Good luck!

Hurling and Shinty

How to play

These are lightning-fast team games popular in Ireland (hurling) and Scotland (shinty), played on large outdoor fields. Similar to hockey, in that players use long sticks with flat blades to pass, dribble and smash a small, hard ball into (or in the case of hurling, over) netted goals found at each end of the field. Where they differ from hockey is that players can hit the ball while it's in the air, and even use their sticks to block and tackle other players. Yikes!

Players

For hurling, thirty – two teams of fifteen.

For shinty, twelve to twenty-four – two teams of six or twelve.

Equipment

Ball – similar in both games, made of cork covered with leather, measuring about 6.5cm in diameter. A little smaller than a tennis ball. In hurling, the ball is called a **sliotar**.
Stick – called a **hurley** in hurling, or a **caman** in shinty. The hurley is about 1m long, and ends in a wide, flat, axe-like blade. The caman looks more or less like a flattened field hockey stick.

Scoring

Teams score points by shooting at the goals. In hurling, the goals have extra uprights extending up from each post, like the H-shaped goals used in rugby. Players have the choice of shooting *over* the goal (and between these posts) for *one point*, or *into* the goal (and past the goalkeeper) for *three points*. Shinty goals are more like standard hockey goals, and players simply shoot into them for one point only.

Hurling and **six-a-side shinty** are both played in two thirty-minute halves. **Twelve-a-side shinty** is played in two forty-five-minute halves, as in football.

4. Balance, Flexibility and Control

Are gymnasts born super-bendy?

Some are, but most are not. Most gymnasts are born just like you and I, but use special exercises to lengthen their muscles, tendons and ligaments, and increase their flexibility over many years.

So they're not all double-jointed, then?

Most aren't, no. In fact, 'double-jointed' people don't really have extra joints at all. They just have unusually flexible tendons and ligaments, which allow their bones to move more freely around each other. So, if you look at it that way, *no* gymnast is double-jointed, because *nobody* is.

Flexibility isn't really about having extra bones or extra-stretchy muscles. It's the ability to *move a body part or joint* *through a wide range of motion*, without being hindered by the surrounding muscles, tendons and other tissues. What's more (and here's the good news if you want to be a top gymnast one day) flexibility is also a **trainable skill**. So even if you're not *born* flexible, you can *become* flexible with the proper training.

Like yoga and stretching and stuff? Doesn't that hurt?

Not if you do it right, no. When people stretch before exercising – or try to stretch their legs or spines in a yoga class – they can overdo it and cause themselves pain and injury. But this is usually because they have the wrong idea about what they're doing.

Flexibility training shouldn't be like putting yourself on a medieval torture rack! Because, if you're training properly, then *you're not actually trying to stretch the muscles* beyond their natural length.

You're not?

Of course not. Do that, and all you'll end up with is a **pulled** or **strained muscle**, or, worse yet, a **torn ligament** or **tendon**. All very nasty injuries.

So what *are* you trying to do when you stretch?

You're trying to *get the brain to reset the length of your muscles and tendons*, which allows them to stretch further before tearing. This, in turn, creates some **slack** in the joints, and leaves the athlete **more flexible**.

To understand how this works, we need to know a bit more about how muscles are **built**.

As we learned in chapter one, a muscle is like a big, meaty bag made of lots and lots of individual **muscle fibres**, all bundled together.

Sure. I remember that much.

Good. OK – now, in turn, each thin muscle fibre contains several bundled **muscle fibrils** (or **myofibrils**), and each muscle fibril contains a bundle of thread-like **myofilaments**. Myofilaments lie side by side within relaxed muscle fibrils, with their ends overlapping.

When they're supplied with energy – plus a signal from an attached nerve – the ends of the myofilaments slide over each other, *increasing the overlap* between them. This shortens the length of the muscle fibrils and fibres of which they form a part, and eventually causes the entire muscle to **contract**.

Not all the fibres in a muscle contract at the same time – some start and end before others. But once all (or most) of the fibres in a muscle have contracted, the muscle is *as short as it can get*, and has reached a state of **maximum contraction**.

But what has all that got to do with stretching?

Well, when you **stretch** a muscle, the *opposite* happens. The thread-like myofilaments are forced to *slide apart*, and the overlap between their ends *decreases* until only a little remains. This (eventually) lengthens the muscle fibrils, fibres and entire muscles that they lie within.

But, once again, the fibres don't all lengthen out at once. Some stretch to their full length before others even begin to lengthen. This is partly because each muscle also contains special stretch-sensors called **muscle spindles**, which lie alongside the fibres within each muscle.

As the spindles are stretched, they *send information* to the spinal cord and brain, telling them how long the muscle has become (or how far it has stretched). This is part of the feedback system we met in the last chapter, and part of what helps the brain build up a picture of where your limbs are and what they're up to – otherwise known as **proprioception**.

Gymnastics

How to play
An individual or team agility sport played in a large indoor gymnasium or arena. Includes a variety of event types, including **floor tumbling**, **vaults**, and complex acrobatics performed on **beams**, **rings**, **high bars** and **pommel horses**. The sport also includes **rhythmic gymnastics**, which is like a cross between gymnastics and ballet, and **trampolining** (more on that later). Gymnasts – or teams of gymnasts – are scored by judging panels on the balance, precision, skill and beauty of their movements.

Players
In most events, gymnasts compete individually, facing other solo gymnasts in a series of vaults or routine attempts. In competitions, the scores of all gymnasts in a school or country's team may be added together to decide the winning team.

Rhythmic gymnastics also features team events, in which teams of two to six athletes perform gymnastic routines all together.

Equipment

Clothing – gymnasts wear form-fitting clothing (leotards for women, vests and leggings for men) that allow free movement while keeping them cool and dry. Many also wear absorbent wristbands and use chalk on their hands to help with grip.

Other gymnastic equipment varies according to the event. This includes:

Floor mats – 12m x 12m areas covered with foam and plastic mats, which cushion feet, hands and tumbling bodies during floor events.

Balance beam – a 5m wooden beam just 10cm in width, set on stands 1.25m off the ground.

Vaulting table, or horse – a leather-covered wood-and-metal saddle raised 1.2–1.3m off the floor on a heavy metal base. Those used in men's vault events are slightly taller than those used in women's.

Parallel bars – two 3.5m steel bars, mounted 0.5m apart, at a height of 2m.

High bar – a single, 2.4m-long steel bar, mounted 2.8m above the ground.

Uneven bars – two 2.4m steel bars, mounted 1.8m apart – one at a height of 2.5m, the other slightly lower, at 1.7m.

Pommel horse – a long, leather-and-plastic saddle with two metal handles on top, mounted on a stand at a height of 1.2m.

Rings – two plastic or metal rings the size of dinner plates, hanging from steel cables at a height of 2.75m.*

Clubs, rope, ribbon, ball, hoop – small, light objects used in rhythmic-gymnastics routines.

---

* The gymnast has to be lifted up to these by a coach before starting the routine.

So why can't you just, you know, stretch your legs into a split all in one go?

Because if a muscle is *stretched too far*, or *too quickly*, then the muscle spindles within them send a different signal to the spinal cord. This triggers a **stretch reflex**, as the spinal cord sends a signal *back* to the overstretched muscle fibres, telling them to **contract**. This done, the fibres tighten up and resist any further attempts to lengthen them. From this point, trying to stretch the muscle any further will only tear and damage the fibres.

So what would happen if I tried to do a full split? Like right now?

You'd probably – ahem – tear a groin muscle.

Oooooooooh. Won't be trying that, then.

Right. If you want to stretch a muscle *safely* and *successfully*, you have to do two things: carefully *lengthen the muscle fibres* themselves, while also *lengthening the muscle spindles*.

If you stretch too far (or too soon), then the stretch reflex kicks in, and you may end up tearing or injuring the muscle. Likewise, if you don't stretch far enough (or for long enough), then the muscle spindles do not lengthen, and the muscle will simply snap back to its original length as soon as you let it go.

Thankfully, there are lots of ways of getting around this problem, and of stretching your muscles *safely* in order to gain flexibility.

Like what?

Gymnasts and other athletes who need flexible muscles

and joints use three basic types of stretching, all of which are useful in different ways:

1. **Static passive flexibility** – you hold a muscle or set of muscles in a stretched position using your bodyweight, or by having someone else stretch you. For example, from a standing position, you could lift your straight leg and put your foot up on a chair. Here, the weight of your own leg does the work of stretching your hamstring and calf muscles.

2. **Static active flexibility** – you stretch a muscle using only the strength or tension in the **opposing muscle** (or the muscle on the other side of the joint or limb). An example of this might be to stand straight and lift one straight leg until it forms a right angle with the other. Here, the **quadricep** muscle on the top of your thigh flexes to lift the leg, which stretches the **hamstring** muscle underneath.

3. Finally, **dynamic flexibility** – you make *forceful movements* that travel through the full range of a joint. For example, performing a swinging **high-kick**, **arm-circle**, or **walk-over back flip**.

All of these work in different ways to increase your flexibility. And with the proper choice of stretching exercise you can make pretty much any part of the body as flexible as you want. So gymnasts and other athletes use a combination of all three of these to gain the flexibility they need for their sports.

One more thing — do you have to be skinny and fit to be flexible?

Nope. It doesn't matter what shape you are, or how good you are at running or swimming, anyone can become more flexible with training. Just give it a go.

Like, now?

Yep. You can try any of the exercises described previously,* or those listed next. Do them all once a day, and you'll be as bendy as a gymnast in no time!

'Hard work has made it easy. That is my secret. That is why I win.'

Nadia Comăneci,
Olympic gymnast, winner of five gold medals and the first gymnast to score a perfect 10.0 in the history of the competition

---

* Although you might want to avoid the back flip – that one's a bit too dangerous to do without help from a gymnastics coach!

Give it a go!

Exercise: gymnastic stretches
Type: isometric
Goal: flexibility

1. **Seal Stretch** – lie face-down on the floor, with your palms either side of your hips. Keeping your legs and the front of your hips on the ground, push with your palms and straighten your elbows. Keep going until your chest is vertical, and you're looking up at the ceiling. For an added challenge, swing both feet upward until your toes are pointed straight up at the ceiling. Hold for twenty to thirty seconds, then slowly lower yourself back to the floor.
Stretches: lower back, hips.

2. **Cat Stretch** – now come to your hands and knees, palms flat on the floor beneath your shoulders, and toes pointed backwards, so that your shins are flat on the ground. Keeping your palms in place, rock your hips backwards until you are sitting on your heels. Your arms should be extended outward, pressed to your ears on each side. Hold for twenty to thirty seconds, then slowly rock back to all fours.
Stretches: lower and upper back, shoulders.

3. **Palm Slide** – now sit up, legs extended out in front, and place your palms on the floor behind you, fingers pointing rearward. Keeping your arms straight, slide your hands backwards along the floor, lowering your upper body towards the floor and stretching the shoulder area. Hold for twenty to thirty seconds, then

slide back up to a seated position.

Stretches: shoulders, chest.

4. **Deep Lunge** – now stand up, placing one foot ahead of the other, and your hands on your hips. Step your forward foot out as far as you can, planting the sole of the front foot on the floor ahead of you, and the knee of the back leg on the floor behind your hips. Push your hips forward until your front and back thighs make a straight line. Hold for twenty to thirty seconds, then rock slowly and carefully back to your feet and switch sides.

Stretches: hips, quadriceps, hamstrings.

5. **Inverted Pike** – now sit down, palms on the floor beside your hips, and both legs straight out in front of you. Rock your upper body backwards, raise your knees towards your chest, rolling back until your knees are over (or, ideally, touching) your chin. Grabbing on to the backs of your ankles for support, extend your knees and straighten your legs. Point your toes, and place them on the floor above your head. Hold for twenty to thirty seconds, then let go of your ankles and slowly roll back to a seated position.

Stretches: lower back, hamstrings, calves.

Gymnastics

How do gymnasts balance on their hands?

In a perfect handstand, Olympic gymnasts look like they're standing still. But every second they spend balancing they're making lots and lots of tiny adjustments with the muscles of their hands, shoulders, stomach, back and legs, just to stay in place.

So they *look* like they're standing still, but actually they're *moving*?

In short, yes. They have to stay in constant motion – making lots of tiny pulls with muscles on every side of their bodies – just to stay upright.

So why doesn't that happen when you stand on your feet?

Actually, it does. Even when you think you're standing still, the muscles of your legs and hips are making constant, tiny adjustments too. If they didn't, you'd start toppling in less than a second.

No way!

See for yourself. Grab a friend, and have them stand in front of you, and place his or her hands on your shoulders. Now have them lift their hands until their fingers and thumbs are *almost* (but not quite) touching the front and back of each shoulder. Their fingers should be no more than a couple of millimetres from the surface of your body.

Now stand as still as you can for two minutes, while your friend attempts to keep their hands *perfectly still*. Pretty soon, you'll find yourself rebounding off your friend's fingers and thumbs, as your body sways around. This shows you that your body, and your friend's body, are making adjustments all the time.

But why does it do that?
It has to. Since we only have two legs (rather than three, like a camera tripod, or four like a table or chair), we have to constantly *balance* on them just to stay upright. It's a bit like a vertical tent pole with guy ropes attached on all sides. The ropes pull the pole in opposing directions to help keep it vertical, and without the ropes it would topple over.

But where are the ropes on a human body?
They're *inside* the body – in the muscles, tendons and other tissues. To stop you toppling forward, you pull with the muscle tendons and tissues of your back and the backs of your legs. To stop you toppling backwards, you pull with the muscles and tissues at the front (or belly) side of your body – the abdominal muscles and the quadricep muscles at the front of your thighs.*

When a gymnast is doing a handstand, a similar thing is happening, except that the hands, arms and shoulders replace the feet, legs and hips.

So why is it so much *harder* to stand on your hands than your feet?
For two main reasons.

Firstly, we humans have **evolved** to stand on our feet.

---

* There are also other muscles involved, like those of your feet, toes, hips and either side of your spine. But you get the basic idea.

Our distant mammalian ancestors walked on all fours like cats and dogs. Our more recent ape-like ancestors walked on their feet and knuckles, much as gorillas and chimpanzees still do today. But around four million years ago, our human-like (or **hominid**) ancestors began walking on their feet alone.

Exactly *where*, *when* and *why* this happened, we're not exactly sure. But one thing's for certain: once they began walking upright, the human race never looked back. Walking on our feet, rather than our hands, allowed us to wade across rivers, to keep a lookout while moving through tall grasses, to carry things as we travelled, to wield tools, to wield weapons, and more. Little wonder, then, that we two-legged, foot-walking humans have done so well for ourselves.

Over time, our bodies became more and more adapted for walking on two feet. Our hip and leg muscles became much more powerful than those of our shoulders and hips. Our heavy skull, neck and back bones became stacked vertically on top of one another, to better align them in a balanced, upright position. And our hearts and blood vessels changed shape to keep blood pumping upward towards the brain, against the pull of gravity. So while we *can* tip upside down and balance on our hands, we're not really *built* to do that. Before long, our shoulder and arm muscles would give out, and we'd become dizzy as blood pressure built up inside the skull.

Secondly, your body has, quite simply, *had a lot more practice balancing on your feet*. Depending on when you first started to stand and walk, you've been doing it since you were about one year old. Although it can eventually become automatic (more about that later), balance is a **skill**.

Balance, in short, is the ability to *control the body's position while stationary or on the move.* So whether you're standing on your feet, hands or head, you have to **learn** how to balance.

Inside the body, balance is sensed and controlled by the **nervous system** and **balance organs**. But, unlike many other senses, balance is *extremely* trainable. And, with practice, almost anyone can pull off quite impressive balancing feats, like headstands and handstands.

So how does that happen?

Balance is basically all about two things: *sensing which way is down,* and *sensing exactly where your muscles are in 3D space.*

Your most important balance-sensing organs lie deep within your ears. Just beside the snail-like **cochlea** of the inner ear, you'll find the **vestibular organs** – a set of three fluid-filled organs that detect the pull of gravity (along with spinning or rotating motions of your head). In short, these organs tell you *which way up* you are at all times, even with your eyes closed.

Your sense of balance also makes use of the special muscle-sensing **proprioceptive** system of the body, combining information from the muscle spindles – plus

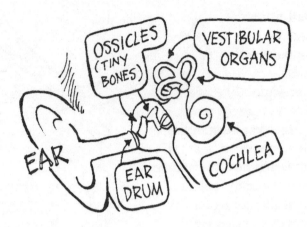

other stretch-sensors within the tendons – to figure out how your arms, limbs, head and body are positioned.

In the brain, signals from the muscles, tendons, ears and eyes are *combined* to create your complete sense – and skill – of balance. As a baby, you use this sense naturally to learn simple balancing skills.

I don't remember learning any of that when *I* was little.

That's because you were too young to remember. But if you're standing and walking today, then you must have learned at some point. And here's how it probably went:

First, you learned how to *sit up* (i.e. balance on your bottom) without toppling over. Later, you learned how to *stand* on your feet while holding on to something (like a table, or a parent's hand) for support. Next, you learned to let go and *balance on two feet* unsupported. Later yet, you learned to *balance on one foot at a time*, and translated that into *walking and running*.

But all those things are so *easy*.

Not for babies, they're not. And, in fact, if you suffer an injury like a badly broken leg, you have to learn to balance and walk all over again once the cast comes off. As with any skill, balancing takes a lot of effort and concentration at first. But after a while balance becomes automatic – part of your on-board **muscle memory**, stored in a part of the brain called the **cerebellum**.

This goes for *simple* balancing skills like standing on one leg, and for more *complex* ones like

walking backwards on a balance beam.

Do *all* gymnasts need a good sense of balance?

Absolutely. It would be impossible to make graceful, balanced movements across a mat or beam without it. In the **pommel horse** and **parallel bars** events, male gymnasts are balancing on their hands throughout the entire, leg-swinging routine. And even in the rings, vault and high-bar events, gymnasts have to keep perfect balance upon landing, or they lose points.

I never thought of that. How *do* you earn points and win in gymnastics? Do the judges measure how far and fast you flip? Or how many times you swing around the bars?

It's not quite as simple as that. In fact, the rules and scoring methods in gymnastics can get a little complicated, as they vary across the different disciplines of gymnastics. But here's the short version:

In **floor** events, gymnasts perform acrobatic balancing and tumbling routines featuring specific moves such as rolls, handsprings, cartwheels, back-flips and somersaults. They are scored for the **difficulty**, **precision** and **beauty** of their moves across the whole floor routine.

Vault events are scored much like diving or trampolining – gymnasts get points for the **take-off**, **mid-air** and **landing** phases of the vault.

On the **rings**, **bars** and **pommel horse**, gymnasts are scored on the **precision** and **beauty** of specific swings and balance positions, on the move used to **dismount** the apparatus, and on the **landing** itself.

In **rhythmic gymnastics**, individuals and teams are scored not only on **precision** and **beauty**, but also the **fluidity** and **grace** of their movements. When using objects like the **ball**, **rope** or **ribbon**, the gymnast must keep the prop in **constant motion** throughout their routine, or face a penalty (and lost points) from the judges.

In general, judges award a maximum of thirty points for each performance – ten points for the **difficulty** of the whole routine (or set of moves attempted), ten points for the **skill** demonstrated in performing these moves and ten for **artistry** – the beauty, fluidity and grace of the routine overall.

Does anyone ever score thirty points?

It has happened, but it's very rare. One of the first to score a full set of perfect 10 scores was fourteen-year-old Romanian gymnast **Nadia Comăneci**, in the Olympic Games of 1976. She's still remembered for this today.

She was only fourteen? How did she manage that?

For one thing, she started gymnastics when she was *four* years old. She was doing cartwheels and balances while most other kids were busy learning how to finger-paint.

Wow. But you know what would've been really impressive . . .

What's that?

If she'd been doing cartwheels *while* finger-painting. Now *that* I'd like to see. That should *totally* be a new gymnastic event.

If you say so . . .

Give it a go!

Exercise: headstands and handstands
Type: static balance
Goal: improve your sense of balance!

1. **Crow Balance** – kneel on the floor, placing your palms next to your knees, fingers apart, and elbows pointing outward. Place the top of your head on the floor a little way ahead of you (if you're on a hard floor, you might want to use a cushion or folded cloth for padding), so that your head and hands form a perfect even-sided (equilateral) triangle. Both elbows should be bent, your upper arms parallel to the floor. Now shift your weight towards your head until your weight is evenly spread between your head and hands. Now lift one knee, and place it on the back of your bent elbow. Now do the same with the other knee. Hold balance for ten to twenty seconds. Try to work up to a full minute!

2. **Headstand** – kneel on the floor, 40–50cm from a wall. Repeat the steps above to get into a crow balance, with both knees propped up on your elbows. Now try extending your legs towards the ceiling, toes first. If you overbalance and your heels touch the wall, don't worry – just push gently off and try to get your legs back to a vertical position. Hold headstand for ten to twenty seconds. Again, try to work up to a full minute. Once you've done that, try doing the headstand away from the wall for ten to twenty seconds. Then work up to doing an unsupported headstand for a full minute.

3. **Supported Handstand** – once you've mastered the unsupported headstand, you can try the supported handstand. Stand facing a wall, bend forward and place your hands on the floor 10cm or so from the wall, shoulder width apart. Keep your arms straight and elbows locked. Now kick your legs up – swinging one straight leg up and over your head while pushing off the floor with the opposite foot. Once both legs are vertical, and your heels are against the wall, hold the position for ten to twenty seconds. Gradually (going for ten more seconds each day), work up to balancing for a full minute against the wall. If you can do that, it's time to join a gymnastics club and learn how to handspring and backflip!

Skiing, Snowboarding, Skating, Skateboarding and Surfing

Why do snowboarders, skateboarders and surfers stand sideways?

*Standing sideways on a snowboard, skateboard or surfboard helps to spread your feet and lower your **centre of mass** or **centre of gravity**. This in turn makes you more stable and balanced as you ride. Standing sideways also helps snowboarders, skateboarders and surfers to tilt and turn their boards.*

How can you lower your centre of gravity? Isn't the Earth the centre of gravity for everyone?

In some ways, yes. But only because the Earth is the most massive thing around. Gravity isn't just a force that pulls things downward. It's a force that attracts *every object in the universe to everything else*. The more massive the object, the stronger the force of its gravitational pull.

We humans fall towards the ground because **human bodies are massive objects** too. Quite simply, the Earth's **centre of mass** (its dense nickel-and-iron **core**) *attracts your body's centre of mass.*

Where's that, then?

It's the point where the weight of the top and bottom

halves of the body are balanced out. Imagine your body as a see-saw – with your heavy head, arms and trunk on one side, and the heavy bones and muscles of your legs on the other. For most people, the point where these two sides balance out is found somewhere *between the hips and the belly-button*. This is the body's own **centre of mass**. You can find your own centre of gravity by trying the 'V-sit' exercise on page 226. Do it right, and you should be able to balance (or even walk!) on your bottom for a minute or more, with very little effort.

When you're sitting or lying on the ground, your centre of mass is as close to the Earth as it can possibly get, and there's little or no need to balance yourself (i.e. make adjustments with your muscles, as we saw in the last section) to stay in place. But the *higher* you lift your centre of mass – and the narrower the base it balances on – the *greater* the need for your *balancing muscles*, and the *less stable* your body becomes.

This is why standing up straight makes you less stable (or more wobbly) than crouching. When you crouch, knees bent, your centre of mass (or belly-button) is lower to the ground.

This is also why balancing on one foot leaves you less stable than standing on two. When you stand on one foot, your body is balanced on a base less than 15cm wide. But when you stand on two feet about hip-width apart, the base supporting your weight is at least double that width, at around 30cm.

Give it a go!

Exercise: V-sit
Type: static balance
Goal: improve core muscle strength and sense of balance

1. Lie flat on the floor, legs straight, arms by your sides.
2. Keeping your back straight, raise your upper body 45° off the floor, letting your arms and hands dangle by your sides.
3. Keeping your legs straight and your knees together, now raise both legs 45° off the floor too. Try to find your 'sit bones' – the hip surfaces at the base of your gluteus maximus (bottom) muscles on which you can balance out the weight of your upper body and legs, like a see-saw.
4. Hold for thirty seconds.
5. Try to work up to a full minute.
6. For an added challenge, try walking forward (and backwards) on your bottom, keeping your legs, hands and upper body off the ground! Go for ten to twenty 'steps' in each direction. This may look a bit weird, but it's a great exercise for strength *and* balance!

Skateboarding

How to play

An agility sport in which individual athletes riding skateboards compete by pulling off the most spectacular jumps, turns and acrobatic 'tricks'. Judges score the skaters' tricks, awarding points for difficulty, originality and style. There are several types of competitive skating events. These include:

Street boarding – this takes place in an arena that simulates an urban (street) area, recreating obstacles such as steps, slopes and rails. Tricks include the **grind** (jumping on to railings and riding them with the middle of the board), the **ollie** (popping the board up into the air to jump up steps or hurdle an object) and the **board flip** (an ollie with added 180°–360° rotation of the board in mid-air).

Half pipe – this takes place on a large, custom-built, U-shaped wooden ramp. Skaters stand on the flat lip of the ramp, then skate down into it, build up speed, roll up the opposite wall and do turns and tricks in mid-air before landing and rolling up the other side. Tricks include **hand plants** (one-handed handstands on the lip of the ramp), **board grabs** (grabbing the board with one hand in mid-air) and **aerials**. Aerials are mid-air acrobatic spins that may go through 360° (one full turn), 540° (1½ turns) or even 720° (that's two full turns!).

Freestyle – here, skaters compete on flat ground, performing tricks without the aid of ramps, jumps or rails. Tricks include **end-overs** (flipping the tail and nose of the board end-to-end while still moving), **finger flips** (popping the board into the air, grabbing the side of the board and flipping it through a full turn before landing) and **pogos** (flipping the board nose up, standing on the wheels and jumping up and down on the tail like a pogo stick!).

Slalom – time-trial events in which skaters race between a series of cones, sometimes pulling tricks and jumps as they do so.

Skateboarding features heavily in the **X Games**, an alternative to the Olympics for wheeled and extreme sports.

Players
One – boarders generally compete solo against other individuals.

Equipment
Skateboard – short, wheeled board typically made of wood, but sometimes plastic or fibreglass. Board length varies, but the 5–6cm front and back wheels are typically set shoulder-width apart for balance.

Helmet – hard plastic helmet that covers the top of the head, protecting the skull from falls on hard ground.

Knee pads, elbow pads, gloves – protect the joints and assist with sliding/handstand tricks.

So is that what skateboarders and surfers do?

By standing with their feet wide apart, and bending their knees to lower their centre of mass, skateboarders, snowboarders and surfers actually do both. The wide stance widens their base of balance, while the bent knees lower their centre of mass. This makes it much easier for them to stay on their boards as they roll along pavements, speed down snowy slopes, and slide along crashing waves.

Standing sideways also helps them to **steer** their boards more easily.

Skateboards, of course, are pretty easy to turn. The skateboarder simply tilts the board to the left or right, by leaning harder on the heels or toes. As the board tilts, it turns the swivelling wheel axles attached to the bottom of the board, and the whole board veers to the left or right. So standing sideways helps give skateboarders the heel-to-toe control they need to tilt their boards.

But snowboards and surfboards don't have axles and wheels.

Right.

So how do you steer one of *those*?

Actually, you steer a snowboard or surfboard in much the same way – by using your toes and heels to tilt the board from side to side. But instead of turning mechanical axles this makes the edges of the board *dig in* to the snow or water, creating **friction** that drags the nose (or tip) of the board from side to side.

Digging the edge of a snowboard into the snow, though, is much tougher work than tilting a skateboard a couple of centimetres up and down. In a fast turn, snowboarders tilt not just their feet, but their *entire bodies* back and forth to drag the board into a turn. Add to this the fact that you're hurtling downhill over a bumpy, uneven surface, and you can see why learning to snowboard involves a *lot* of time spent falling on your bottom.

And that's just in the racing (or downhill) snowboard events.

There's more than one type of snowboarding event?

Yep. Actually, there are several. **Downhill**, **slalom** and **giant slalom** snowboarding events are played and scored in much the same way as their counterparts in skiing, with the exception of **four-cross racing**, in which up to four athletes race downhill over a course filled with bumps, jumps and obstacles.

But **freestyle snowboarding** takes place in an extended, snow-covered **half-pipe ramp**, similar to those used in skateboarding and BMX, only far longer and angled downhill so that boarders can build up speed as they traverse it.

As they slide up the vertical walls of the ramp and fly into the air, the boarders perform tricks at each turn, working their way down the half-pipe in a series of spectacular spins, flips and aerial manoeuvres. Tricks include **board grabs** (grabbing the board with one hand in mid-air), **180° spins** (landed with the boarder riding forward),

360° spins (landed with the boarder riding backwards) or **combinations** of these.

To pull these tricks off successfully, freestyle snowboarders have to shift their *whole bodies* (and boards) around their centre of mass as they fly and flip through the air. This, as you may imagine, takes a *lot* of practice.

Snowboarding

How to play

An agility sport, similar to skiing, that takes place on sloped courses (or **pistes**) covered with real or artificial snow. Athletes manoeuvre using flat wooden or fibreglass snowboards, clipped on to special boots that bind the board to their feet. But, unlike skiers, snowboarders ride sideways – more like skateboarders or surfers. Event types are similar to skiing. These include **downhill**, **slalom** and **giant slalom snowboarding**, where athletes race downhill through flagged gates, and **freestyle snowboarding**, where athletes on boards perform jumps and tricks off skateboard-style half-pipe ramps.

Players
One to four – in most events, boarders compete individually, but in some events – like **snowboard cross** – up to four boarders tackle the same slope, racing each other to the bottom.

Equipment
Snowboard – short, flexible board with rounded edges, made of fibreglass and/or plastic polymers with steel edging. The flexible boot-bindings are a little different to those of skis, and are arranged so that both toes face the same edge of the board, surfer-style.* Boards vary in length from 1.5–2.2m – longer boards are used for downhill racing, shorter boards for slalom and freestyle events.
Ski boots – foam-lined boots with locking buckles and bindings – similar to those used in skiing.
Padded jacket and trousers – protect against impact on hard ice and snow. Falls are more common in snowboarding than skiing, so these can be essential.
Goggles, helmet – similar to those worn in skiing, used for the same reasons.

---

* In fact, the first snowboards were developed by surfers looking for something to do in the winter months when surf season was over!

What about surfboards? How tricky are they to turn?

Turning a surfboard is even *tougher* to do. At least without falling off in the process. Once a surfer has paddled out and caught a crashing wave, he or she turns the board side-on to the wave, digging one edge of the board into it at all times. This prevents the board from slipping down the wave, where the surfer loses speed and risks '**wiping out**' (falling off, with a heavy wave crashing overhead).

Keeping this balance is *extremely* difficult, so surfers place their feet wide apart on the board, and bend their knees deeply as they drive the board into turns. Without this wide, low base on the board, they couldn't hope to stay on the wave for long. Beginners at surfing sometimes start their training with a **bongo board** or **rocker board** – a home-made see-saw-like device that helps to train balance on dry land before they get into the water. (If you want to make your own, see the exercise at the end of this section.)

Skilled surfers, though, get so good at maintaining this balance that they can carve their way into turns at will – swinging the tip of the board towards the crest of a wave, then swinging it back round to avoid flipping over the top. Top surfers even fly off the wave, turn in mid-air and land back on the same wave with ease.

Is that how they win in competitions? By doing lots of flips and turns on the wave?

Well, in official competitions, surfers take to the waves in groups of two or four, competing in head-to-head contests or **heats**. Each heat takes around twenty minutes, during which judges score each surfer based on **how many waves** they caught, **how difficult** the wave was to ride, **how long** they rode each wave *and* the **quality of tricks and turns** they pulled off while riding. At the end of each heat, points are added, the two lowest-scoring surfers are dismissed and the top two progress to the next round.

Whoa. Sounds tough.

It is. But the hardest part is mastering that first, basic, **side-on surfing position**. Once you can ride a wave naturally and without thinking, adding turns and tricks becomes fairly simple. (Or so I'm told . . .)

‘It's all about where your mind is at.’

Kelly Slater,
eleven-times World Champion in competitive surfing

Hang on a minute — I just had a thought. *Skiers* don't ride their skis sideways. They just hurtle down the slope facing forward. Why's that?

You're right – skiers do face forward. But that's when they just want to go *down* the slope. When they want to turn or slow down, skiers have to dig the edge of their skis into

Surfing

How to play

An agility sport in which players balance on long, streamlined boards and ride rolling, breaking waves. Surfers are awarded points by judges for how long they stay with the wave and for the various turns, tricks and jumps they pull off while riding.

Players

One – surfers compete individually, but in competitions up to four surfers may paddle out to ride waves at the same time, so that judges can compare their skill and technique.

Equipment

Surfboard – long, tapering, wooden or fibreglass boards, with fins on the underside of the tail end for stability in the water. Surfboards vary in length from 1.8m shortboards to 2.75m longboards. Longboards are more stable and easier to ride, but shortboards are more manoeuvrable, and can make tighter turns.

Wetsuit – skintight neoprene suits that trap a layer of warm water near the skin and keep the surfer warm during long periods in the ocean. Some surfers also wear nylon tights under their wetsuits to protect against jellyfish stings.

the snow and swing round sideways too.

Slalom skiers, who have to ski round poles or through gates, must learn to do this quickly and skilfully if they are to make it through a course without missing one. And even downhill skiers and ski jumpers need to be able to turn and stop once they reach the bottom!

You know — that's one question that's always niggled me . . .

What's that?

What kind of total *nutter* invented the ski jump? I mean, how crazy would you have to be to try that for the first time?!!

Well, no one knows for sure who invented it, but some say it was Olaf Rye – a Norwegian soldier who launched himself over 9m for a bet in 1809, in the Norwegian mountain village of Morgedal. From there, it became popular throughout Norway, and was eventually added to the list of Winter Olympics events in 1924. Now, the ski-jump record stands at over 240m – almost fives times the length of a standard Olympic swimming pool.

**Like I said.
Nutters . . .**

Give it a go!

Exercise: build your own bongo board
Type: dynamic balance
Goal: improve sense of dynamic balance

1. Grab (or get a friend or family member to buy) two items from a local DIY shop: a thick wooden board measuring 60cm x 30cm (it should be thick and sturdy enough to hold your full bodyweight) and a piece of hard, thick plastic pipe at least 30cm long, and 15cm in diameter.
2. If you can, cover the pipe in a single layer of grip tape (the kind you get for tennis-racquet handles) for extra friction.
3. Lay the pipe on a flat surface, and place the board on top like a see-saw.
4. Place a foot on each end of the board, then try to kick off and balance in the middle (without letting either end of the board touch the floor) for as long as possible. Start with ten seconds of balancing, then work up to a full minute. Once you can balance for three minutes or more, you'll be ready for skating or surfing in no time!

Skiing/Ski Jump

How to play

An agility sport that takes place on sloped courses (or **pistes**) covered with real or artificial snow. Athletes manoeuvre using long skis made of wood and composite materials, clipped on to special boots that bind the skis to their feet. In **downhill** and **slalom** skiing, skiers race downhill through flagged gates, trying to get through the gates and reach the bottom of the course in the shortest time possible. In **freestyle** skiing, athletes on skis perform jumps and tricks, which are scored by judges for difficulty, originality and style. In **ski jump**, solo skiers hurtle down a long, curving take-off ramp, leap off the end and try to travel as far as possible before making a safe landing.

Players

One – skiers usually compete individually, against the clock or against one another.

Equipment

Skis – long, flat strips made of wood, fibreglass and/or plastic polymers, narrower towards the centre, and wider towards the ends. In the centre of each ski are the **bindings** – releasable clamps that lock on to the toe and heel of a ski boot and hold it in place. Different lengths of ski are selected for different types of events. Downhill skis, at 2m, are the longest and fastest. Slalom skis, at 1.5–1.9m are shorter but more agile – ideal for tight turns.

Ski boots – hard plastic, foam-lined boots with locking buckles that secure them on the foot, and solid plastic plates on the sole, which slide into the locking bindings on each ski.

Ski poles – tubular plastic or aluminium poles with hand

grips, which help skiers to maintain their balance as they lean their bodies from side to side. These are not used in ski jump, as they could cause injury upon landing.

Goggles – foam and plastic goggles with wide, clear plastic lenses. These keep wind and snow out of the eyes, like miniature car windscreens.

Speed suit – smooth, Lycra, one-piece bodysuits* that cut down on air resistance and increase speed.

Helmet – foam and plastic crash helmet worn to protect the skull during high-speed crashes.

Rules

In the **downhill**, **slalom** and **giant slalom** racing events, the rules are more or less the same. Skiers have one attempt** to get to the bottom of a course as quickly as possible, skiing round single flagposts or between pairs of double-flagged gates on the course as they do so. Missing even one flag or gate results in instant disqualification.

The main differences between these three types of event are the steepness of the slope and the number and position of gates on the course.

In **downhill racing**, the slope is very steep, but the gates are few and far between, and are arranged to allow the skier to follow a fairly straight line through the course.

In **slalom skiing**, the course is shorter and the slope shallower. But there are fifty to eighty gates arranged throughout the course, requiring the skier to make lots of sharp zigzagging movements in order to complete the course.

---

* Racing skiers never wear the bulky jackets and trousers (sallopettes) seen on tourist ski resorts. So if you see a skier in a skin-tight suit, he or she is probably a professional. Either that or a serious poser.

** Or sometimes two, in which case the times are added for the two runs.

Giant slalom is similar to slalom, only the course is longer, and the gates are arranged so that not all of them require a turn in order to pass through.

Freestyle skiing features two quite different types of event. **Mogul racing** sees pairs of skiers racing each other down a bumpy slope, passing through course gates while trying to beat the other to the bottom. **Aerial freestyle** is scored more like diving, trampolining, or freestyle BMX (see later). Here, skiers thunder down a slope towards a curving ramp, then launch themselves into the air and perform aerial acrobatics – twists, turns, somersaults, etc. – before landing. Judges score their tricks based on difficulty, originality, form and style, adding the scores over several 'jumps' to determine the final winner.

In **ski jump**, competitors take turns to jump one at a time, aiming to reach one of two lines marked in the snow, at distances of 90m or 120m from the take-off point. In competition, jumpers lose points for every metre by which they miss the target line. They are also awarded points for style, and docked points for sloppy jump technique or crash-landings. The points are awarded by five judges who sit in a tall tower to one side of the take-off ramp. The jumper with the most points after several jumps wins.

Diving, Trampolining and Synchronized Swimming

How many somersaults can a high-diver do?

That depends how high the diving platform is, and whether the diver wants to slip gracefully into the water at the end of it, or just 'bomb it', feet or back first. In theory, a diver leaping from a 10m platform could pull five or more somersaults in a row before hitting the water. But, in practice, divers rarely go for more than three.

Why not? Wouldn't they get more points for more somersaults?

Probably not. While diving judges *do* score dives for difficulty, they also score them for other things too.

Like what?

In professional diving competitions, each athlete dives five to six times (in **Olympic** diving events, it's six times for men, five times for women), and judges score each dive for **skill**, **performance** and **beauty**. Separate scores are given for the **take-off**, **flight** and **landing** (entry) phases of the dive, with marks being deducted for imperfect leaps, imperfect limb movements and splash-landings.*

The judges then multiply this by another number which depends on the **difficulty** of the dive to get the final score. A two-and-a-half forward somersault with twist, for

---

* The perfect landing makes no splash at all, and is called a *rip*. This is what all divers aim for.

example, would be multiplied by a larger number than a single forward somersault with tuck.

So the more somersaults they do, the bigger the score, right?

Not if they don't perform them perfectly in the air, or splash into the pool at the end of the dive. Pulling a perfect **four-and-a-half somersault** is a *lot* harder than pulling a perfect **two-and-a-half somersault with twist**. The former is likely to end with a big splash, earning you zero points for skill, performance and beauty. And 4.5 multiplied by zero is still zero.

Are the judges really that strict?

Yep. Judges not only look at the movement your body

makes during a dive, but also the **shape**. In diving, there are three basic positions. These are:

Straight – the whole body is stiff and straight from neck to toe-tips.

Tuck – the body is balled up, holding the knees to the chest.

Pike – the body is bent forward, legs straight, with elbows round knees.

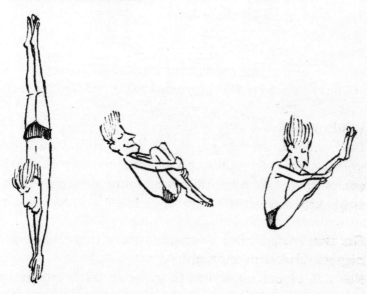

How and **when** the divers enter and emerge from these positions during the dive will decide most of their score. At the end of the five or six dives, the points for each dive are totalled, and the athletes with the highest scores either advance to the next heat or win the competition outright.

And, usually, it's the divers who made the cleanest, most beautiful-looking dives that win, rather than the ones who pulled the highest number of somersaults.

Diving

How to play

An agility sport played in a deep diving or swimming pool, in which athletes leap from raised platforms or springboards and perform acrobatics in the air before sliding head first into the water. Judges award points for the difficulty and performance of each dive, and the points are added to decide the winner.

Players

For standard diving events, one – athletes dive solo.

For synchronized diving, two – athletes dive in pairs.

Equipment

Pool – some diving events are held at the deep end of standard swimming pools, but most professional competitions are held at custom-built diving pools. In either case, the depth of the water must be at least 2m for springboard dives, and 3.5m for 10m high-dives.

Platform/springboard – springboard divers leap from flexible wooden or aluminium springboards with non-slip surfaces, placed 1m or 3m above the surface of the water. For high-diving events, divers climb steps to leap from solid platforms at a height of 5m or 10m above the water.

But how do divers stop somersaulting and twisting once they've started?

What d'you mean?

OK — let's say you want to do two-and-a-

half somersaults with a single twist. How do you stop there, and avoid spinning on into extra twists and somersaults?

Good question. In fact, divers mostly do this with the *movement of their arms* while they're in the air.

When a diver wants to start a somersault, he or she does what is called a '**throw**'. To begin a **forward somersault**, you raise your arms above your head and throw your elbows down and to the front. This motion carries your upper body forward, and starts the somersault. From there, **tucking** (or curling your knees to your chest) *increases* your rotation speed, while pulling your body out straight will *decrease* it.

What if you want to do a *backwards* somersault instead?

To begin a **backwards somersault**, you start with a **reverse throw**. This involves crouching down a little, and lowering your arms to your sides, then throwing your hands and elbows back, up, and over your shoulders as you straighten up. This motion carries your upper body rotating backwards. Once again, **tucking** after take-off increases the speed of that backwards rotation, and straightening out will slow the rotation, so that you can stop somersaulting.

By throwing, tucking and straightening at *precisely* the right times, a diver can start or stop rotating at will, and control how many somersaults he or she performs.

What about twists? How do you start and stop those?

By *throwing* one arm up, and the other arm down, like this:

This arm motion starts the upper body twisting, and the hips and legs soon follow. By bending the elbows, the diver can speed up the twist, and by straightening the elbows, the diver slows it down.

Cool! Can you use the same tricks on a trampoline?

Absolutely. **Divers** and **trampolinists** actually have a lot in common, and use many of the same methods to control their bodies in the air. The positions and moves are similar to those used in diving – **straight**, **pike**, **tuck**, **twist**, **somersault** and so on. And just like divers, trampolinists lose points for imperfect arm, leg and body positions during moves.*

The big difference, of course, is that trampolinists get to make a whole series of '**jumps**', one after the other. And, while divers always land head first, trampolinists can land on their chest, back *or* feet. This means trampolinists can attempt things divers *cannot* do, such as **quarter**

---

* Trampolinists must also keep their *legs together* and *toes pointed* throughout their entire routine, and points are deducted if both feet fail to land on the trampoline at *exactly the same time*. Harsh!

somersaults, which end flat on the back, or **three-quarter back somersaults**, which end chest down. Try that in the pool, and all you'll get is a painful belly-flop or back-slap.

So do the judges watch every single bounce, and score every move a trampolinist makes? How do they keep up with it all?

Well, in competitions trampolinists 'prepare' the judges by giving them a *list of ten moves* they will attempt during their routines. They can attempt these in any order, and they're free to simply bounce up and down between the official moves. But *all ten moves must be completed* before the athlete comes to a halt.

There is no time limit on the routine, but at the end of it the athlete *must* come to a perfect **two-footed standing stop** on the canvas. If they fail to do this, they lose points. At the end of each routine, the points are added, and the winning athletes progress to the next round, or win the competition outright.

Wow. And I thought trampolining was an easy sport. Just a bit of bouncing up and down.

Nope. It's a very tough sport, requiring lots of strength (especially in the legs and back) and very precise movements. Throw your arms or tuck your body a quarter-second too late, and your somersault is going to look pretty ugly.

But the good news is that if you can master these movements you'll be a whizz at other sports too.

In **gymnastic vault** events, you're somersaulting and

Trampolining

How to play

An agility sport played in an indoor gymnasium or arena, in which athletes bounce into the air using a sprung trampoline, performing aerial acrobatics such as twists, pikes and somersaults. Judges score the athletes on the skill, difficulty and precision of each movement.

Players

One to two – in most trampolining events, athletes compete individually. But in **synchronized trampolining**, pairs of athletes compete at the same time.

Equipment

Trampoline – sprung canvas sheet attached to a heavy metal frame by springs, and surrounded by foam padding that prevents the trampolinist from injury. The central canvas measures 4 x 2m, but athletes try to stay right in the centre of the 2 x 1m 'jumping zone' in its middle.

twisting using the same techniques – you just need to do it all very quickly. In **skydiving**, you can tuck, straighten and position your arms for twists and somersaults in mid-air, and you have plenty of time to do it. (Well, until it's time to pull the ripcord for your parachute, anyway!) Even **synchronized swimmers** use similar techniques and motions to flip and twist underwater.

Really? You can do underwater somersaults?

Absolutely.

How does that work?

Well, positioning your arms and tucking your body works in the water too. So synchro swimmers use these methods to help rotate and twist themselves into position. But rather than 'throw' themselves into manoeuvres, synchro athletes push and tread at the water with their arms and legs.

In fact, the first thing you learn as a synchro swimmer is how to move or hold your position in the water with the legs alone, using water-treading **eggbeater kicks**. Next you learn **sculling**, or manoeuvring and treading water with the hands and arms. Then you combine the two, and start exploring how to twist, flip and somersault like underwater trampolinists.

Once a *whole team* has mastered these moves, they can then arrange themselves into patterns to perform specific moves and routines. This is where the *real* fun begins.

There are a limited number of recognized 'move' types in synchro. The basic moves include:

Platform lifts – one swimmer is raised and held clear of the water by the others, who float beneath the surface.

Stacked lifts – one or more swimmers stand on the shoulders of the others, with both lifters and liftees raised above the surface.

Throws – one or more swimmers are thrown clear of the surface by the others, clearing the surface completely like a breaching dolphin before landing gracefully back in the water.

You get to throw each other about in the pool?
Yep.

Smart! I usually get thrown out by a lifeguard when I start doing that kind of thing . . .
Next time, just keep it graceful, and tell him you're practising for the Olympics.

Nahh. That won't work.
Why not?

I already tried that with the snorkel, remember?
Oh, yeah. So you did.

Give it a go!

Exercise: synchro flips
Type: skill
Goal: improve dexterity and agility in the water

Pike Flip

1. Begin by treading water, feet down, your head above the surface.
2. While scooping water upward and forward with both hands, dive your head forward and underwater, pointing the top of your head to the bottom.
3. Keeping both legs straight and your feet together, let your hips rise out of the water until the backs of your legs are level with the surface.
4. Keep scooping (sculling) the water towards your face, rotating your head right under as your hips dip below the surface.
5. Bend your knees towards your chest, then scoop water behind you with both hands to stop your head from popping up too quickly.
6. Finally, extend your feet towards the bottom, and wait for rapturous applause.

Back flips

1. Begin by lying flat out on the surface, face up.
2. Scoop your arms out to your sides underwater, then force yourself backwards and underwater by pushing your hands overhead.
3. Tuck your knees to your chest and make yourself into the smallest ball possible.
4. Flip yourself over backwards by pushing the water over your head.
5. Bring your knees right over your head and towards the bottom of the pool.
6. Extend both feet towards the bottom and surface for applause, or tip backwards and go for another one!

Synchronized Swimming

How to play
A water sport, also known as **synchro**, in which pairs or teams of athletes perform graceful, dance-like movements in a deep swimming pool, accompanied by music. Much like rhythmic gymnastics, only in the water. Teams are awarded points for the precision, beauty and difficulty of their movements, and for their ability to move and perform as one.

Players
Two or eight. Synchro swimmers compete as pairs (duets) or teams of eight.

Equipment
Pool – a standard swimming pool, although competition pools may also have underwater cameras, to show movements going on beneath the surface.
Noseclip – stops water going up the nose when the swimmers submerge backwards or invert their bodies in the water. Some swimmers also wear earplugs.

Downhill Biking and BMX

How do you make a bike jump?

*Sport bikers do this in one of two ways. The first is to make the bike '**bunnyhop**', by pressing their weight down into the pedals and hopping into the air, bringing the bike up with them. The second way is to ride the bike off a shallow, steep or even vertical ramp – launching the bike and rider up to 15m into the air!*

15 metres? Seriously?
Yep. American BMX champs **Mat Hoffman** and **Kevin Robinson** have both jumped BMX bikes to heights of over 15m. That's more or less the same height as a six-storey building.*

How did they get that high?
For starters, they jumped from specially designed, U-shaped, **half-pipe ramps** with curving walls over 8m

---

* Who needs lifts and stairs when you've got a BMX, eh? Definitely a more enjoyable way to get to work in the morning . . .

tall. Rolling down one near-vertical wall helped them to gather the speed and momentum they needed to thunder up the other wall and launch themselves more than 7m off the top of the ramp. Then they tilted and turned their bikes in mid-air, angling the front wheels back downward, so that they could land and roll safely back down the ramp on the way down.

So did they do it just for a laugh, or do they do that kind of thing all the time?

Both riders did it to break the previous world record for the *highest jump on a BMX*. (Robinson actually broke his friend Hoffman's record, which he had set fifteen years before). But, actually, both are also **BMX Freestyle** athletes – world champions in ramp-jumping events.

They have bike-jumping events? Like in the Olympics and stuff?

Not in the Olympics, no. At least not *yet*.

But vertical ramp riding (or **vert**) events are part of most **BMX Freestyle competitions**, and are a regular feature of extreme sports competitions like the **X Games**. There, BMX Freestyle events are divided into five basic types:

Street BMX events – take place in an arena with specially arranged obstacles similar to those found in towns and cities, such as steps, slopes and rails. Riders earn points for performing tricks like **rail slides** (sliding along rails using the bike frame alone) and **bunnyhops** (hopping both wheels of the bike up steps or over obstacles).

Park BMX events – similar, but also use larger, wooden ramps like those used in skateboard parks. This

Freestyle BMX

How to play

An agility sport in which individual athletes riding BMX bicycles compete by pulling off the most spectacular jumps, tricks and balances. Judges score the riders' tricks, awarding points for difficulty, originality and style.

Players

One – riders compete solo.

Equipment

BMX – lightweight Bicycle Motocross (BMX) bicycle, often customized with special seats, handlebars and wheel-axle pegs to allow the rider to pull off more spectacular tricks.

Ramps, trails and jumps – custom-built dirt mounds, wooden ramps, U-shaped half-pipes and steel rails, used by riders to pull off jumps, flips and slides.

Helmet and pads – hard plastic helmet, knee pads and elbow pads, which protect the skull and joints from injury in the event of a crash or *wipeout*.

expands the range of tricks to include **jumps** and **aerials**, in which riders spin their handlebars or flip their entire bike in mid-air.

Vert events –take place solely on large, half-pipe ramps, and riders roll back and forth, up and down, pulling tricks in mid-air as they jump off the vertical ends of the ramp. Tricks include **lip grinds** (rail sliding along the upper edge of the ramp) and full **backwards somersaults**! This is the type of event in which Mat Hoffman and Kevin Robinson would compete.

Trail events – involve jumping (and pulling tricks) off one or more large **dirt ramps**. The aerial tricks are similar to those seen in **park** and **vert** events.

Flatland events – held on flat, open concrete courts, and riders have to improvise tricks *without* the assistance of ramps, rails or jumps.

Many say that this is the hardest of the five types of event, since there's nothing but the bike to work with. Flatland freestylers become experts at hopping and jumping their bikes into the air from a standing start. Other common tricks include **wheelies** (popping the front wheel up), **endos** (popping the back wheel up), **peg stands** (riding or balancing on the axle pegs, often combined with a wheelie or endo) and **fakies** (riding backwards, seated on the handlebars).

But how can the riders make their bikes hop and jump without ramps?

The basic move is called a **bunnyhop**. In terms of physics, bunnyhopping a bike is just the same as hopping or jumping on the spot *without* a bike.

How's that?

Well, think for a second about what happens when you hop or jump into the air. First, you bend your knees. This builds pressure and tension in your legs, and lengthens the muscles of the thighs and calves, in preparation for the jump.

Next, you *contract* your **quadricep** and **calf muscles**, which causes your feet to press down on the ground. Since every action has an equal and opposite reaction, the *ground pushes back on your feet*, lifting them (temporarily) off the ground.

If you keep your legs straight after take-off, then your feet will lift 30cm or so off the ground before gravity pulls you back down again.

But if, right after take-off, you start contracting your **hamstring muscles**, then this draws your feet upward towards your hips, and your feet are lifted a metre or more off the ground.

OK — but how does it work on a bike?

More or less the same way. The only difference is that you're standing on the bike pedals (and holding on to the handlebars) instead of the ground. This, in effect, puts a *springy bike frame*, two *springy wheels*, and two *springy tyres* between your feet and the ground.

To start a bunnyhop, the rider bends his (or her) knees, which increases the tension in the frame and wheels, and increases the pressure in the tyres. The tyres then push into the ground and, as the ground pushes back, the tyres, wheels and frame **rebound** into the air. If the rider keeps his legs straight, the tyres will lift a few centimetres off the ground. But if he draws his feet to his hips the bike will be *drawn up with them*, and the tyres will hop much higher.

Cool!

That's not all. By shifting his weight back and forth – and pulling up on the handlebars with his hands – the rider can make the bike jump up, front wheel first, back wheel second. By doing this, he not only gets more height, but can also hop the wheels, one at a time, over or on to an obstacle. This comes in handy for mounting rails and raised ramps in **street** and **park** BMX events.

Would that work on a normal bike, or do you need a BMX bike to do it?

Well, it's easier to do on a BMX, since they're built with lighter, springier frames than other types of bike. But mountain bikers also pull jumps and bunnyhops to clear obstacles in **downhill** and **4X mountain biking events**.

What are they, then?

They're special **racing** events in which riders on mountain bikes start at the top of a rugged outdoor course, and at the starting signal make their way to the bottom as quickly as possible.

Most events feature jumps or obstacles, which have to be cleared or rounded – like the flags used in slalom skiing. Often, bikers must jump their bikes over bumps and ramps just to make it to the next flag without slowing down. This is where bunnyhopping and jumping come in handy. Many mountain bikers also have special shoes that clip on to their pedals, which help them to lift the frame into the air during a jump.

In **standard downhill**, riders race solo against the clock, trying to get the fastest time possible. But in **4X racing**, riders start side by side at the top of a course, and the winner is the first to make it to the bottom.

That sounds *brilliant*! Why isn't *that* in the Olympics?

Well, a lot of people are *asking* for it to be added. So maybe one day it will be. Better start working on your bunnyhops, just in case . . .

Give it a go!

Exercise: BMX tricks
Type: skill
Goal: improve dexterity and balance

Wheelie (easy)

1. Ride up a slight slope, pedalling straight and SLOWLY.
2. Stand on the pedals and shift your hips over the back wheel.
3. Pull up on the handlebars to lift the front wheel into the air. Not too high – just 30cm or so off the ground at first.
4. If you start to tip up too far, just lean forward to drop the front wheel down again.
5. Keep the wheelie under control for three to five seconds, then drop the front wheel to the ground.
6. Now try the same sequence on flat ground.

Endo (hard)

1. Ride down a slight slope, steering straight and going SLOWLY.
2. Stand on the pedals, shift your hips towards the front wheel and gently pull the front brake.
3. Allow the rear wheel to pop off the ground a little. Again – not too high. You don't want to fall forward over the handlebars.
4. Hold for a second or two, then release the brake and shift your hips backwards to land the back wheel.
5. Now try the same sequence on flat ground.

Bunnyhop (very hard)

1. Begin by rolling (not pedalling) SLOWLY on flat ground, steering straight.
2. Stand on the pedals, and quickly shift your hips backwards, a little behind the seat.
3. Pull back on the handlebars to get the front wheel off the ground.
4. Immediately shift your hips upward and forward. You're basically jumping into the air with your hips.
5. As you do so, keep your feet in contact with the pedals, but lift your feet up with your hips, rather than press down into the pedals. This will bring the bike up into the air with you.
6. Bend your knees and tuck them to your chest to get maximum height.
7. Don't expect to hop more than a few centimetres on your first try. Even the experts have trouble bunnyhopping higher than 30cm, so 10cm or so isn't bad at all!
8. Gravity will bring your bike back to the ground, free of charge.

Downhill Mountain Biking

How to play

A racing sport in which individual athletes ride custom-built off-road racing bikes through a downhill course as quickly as possible. Much like downhill skiing, only on mountain bikes rather than skis.

Players

In **standard downhill** biking, one – riders compete solo, against the clock.

In **4X downhill** biking, four riders compete to race downhill through the same course at the same time.

Equipment

Downhill bike – custom-built, lightweight mountain bike with steel suspension springs added to the frame or forks to absorb shock from the wheels. Most also have special pedals that attach to the rider's shoes, but detach spontaneously during a crash, like ski bindings.

Helmet – lightweight plastic-and-foam cycle helmet, worn to protect the skull during crashes.

Gloves – worn for extra grip on the handlebars.

Bobsleigh and Luge

How do you steer a toboggan?

*That depends on the type of toboggan you're riding. In a four-man or two-man **bobsleigh**, a single driver steers with a pair of cables that swivel the blades beneath him, while the others lean their bodies into each turn. On a one-man **luge** or **skeleton**, the rider does it by shifting weight and dragging or pushing with the legs.*

So you can steer a toboggan?
Of course you can! What did you think they did, just jump on and hope?

Why not? That's how I ride my sledge down snowy hills.
Good grief. It's wonder you're still alive.

There are different kinds of toboggan too?
Yep – and several kinds of tobogganing event. When most people think 'tobogganing', they think of a four-man **bobsleigh**. And bobsleighing (or **bobsledding**, as it's also known) is the oldest of the Winter Olympics tobogganing events.

Bobsledding is a team event in which teams of two or four powerful sprinters push a bobsleigh on to the ice-covered **run**, and work together to steer it through the twists and turns as quickly as possible.

Today, almost all competition bobsleigh runs are covered with so-called 'artificial' ice. This is ice that is not naturally formed, but pressure-formed on the track surface. Artificial ice is produced using a process of compressing **ammonia** or **freon gas**, and then allowing it to expand and cool. This cooling process removes heat from water hosed over the track. The thick, even layer of ice this produces is much safer for bobsleds, luges and skeletons to race on, as it contains fewer lumps, bumps and cracks that could bounce the craft into the air, or send them spinning over the track walls.

Right. So who steers, and how?

The pilot in a bobsleigh sits at the front, holding on to a pair of ring-like handles attached to cables or ropes. Pulling on these cables swivels the front axle of the bobsleigh, upon which two of the four steel blades (or **runners**) are mounted. By pulling the handles, the driver controls how far up the walls of the run the bobsleigh goes – seeking to find the fastest possible path (or **racing line**) through the run.

But, in a sense, it's not *just* the driver who steers a bobsleigh. *Everyone* does.

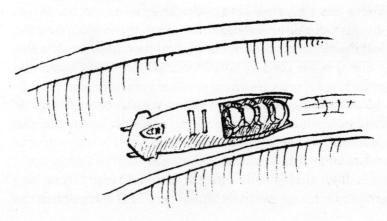

What do you mean?

At first the sledders have to work together just to *get the sled moving* at a decent speed. Later, they have to work together to *control the speed* of the sled, and to *stop it from flipping over* as it races up the walls of the run.

At the beginning of a run, the sledders move their sleigh to a starting line at the top of the run, holding on to bars that protrude from the sides of the craft, and shuffling it back and forth in anticipation of the 'go' signal. At the signal, they push and sprint as fast as possible to get the sled up to speed. Within 50m, they all have to be inside the sled, so they push as long as they can, then jump in one by one (front to back) and prepare to enter the run's first turn.

OK. *Then* what?

From this point on, the **driver** steers, the **brakeman** controls the speed and *all* (including, in a four-man bobsleigh, the two middle passengers) *lean their bodies* to assist with turning at speed.

Why do they need to do that?

Because of the **centrifugal forces** that fling the sled out and up as it rounds each curve. You feel these same forces when you sit on a spinning roundabout. The faster the roundabout turns, the more you feel yourself flung towards the *outside* of it. If you can't keep a good enough grip on the roundabout, you'll slip and fly off it as the roundabout spins on.

A similar thing happens when a bobsleigh enters a fast turn. The sled speeds into the banked turn, attempting to follow its curved path. But centrifugal forces push the sled towards the outside of the curve, and up the banking walls of the run. If the sled enters a turn too fast, the friction of the runners against the ice will be overcome, and the sled will slide too far up the wall and flip over. Or, worse yet, fly right over a curving wall, something you really don't want to do while travelling at over 100mph (150km/h).

Yikes! That sounds a bit more perilous than sledging!

It is. But, on the flipside, if the sled *slows too much* on the turns, the team will lose the race. So bobsleigh isn't just about running and holding on while one guy or girl steers through the run. It's a constant, dangerous, *balancing act* by all the sledders.

What about the luge and the skeleton, then? What are they?

The one-man and two-man **luge** is much simpler to look at, but far more difficult (and dangerous!) to drive. It's basically a flat plastic seat with two metal runners underneath, which curve upward at the front end to form two **steering bows**. The luge athlete lies with his or her back on the seat, holds on to the sides and steers by pressing his/her legs against the outsides of the steering bows.

With just one or two people on board (and to accelerate it at the beginning), a luge can't reach the same speed as a bobsleigh. But lying flat on your back racing down an icy run at **75–100mph (120–160km/h)** is terrifying enough . . .

Bobsleigh (Bobsled)

How to play

A high-speed winter sport, also known as **bobsledding**, in which teams of athletes sprint to push a long, aerodynamic bobsleigh on to an ice-covered track (or **run**), then jump in and steer it through banking twists and turns, trying to reach the finish as quickly as possible.

Players

In two-man bobsleigh events, two men or women per sleigh; in four-man bobsleigh (you guessed it) four per bobsleigh. Sleighs (or sleds) make the runs one at a time.

Equipment

Bobsleigh – also called a **bobsled**, or simply **sled**. A long, submarine-like fibreglass sled mounted on four steel blades or **runners**. Two-man sleds are up to 2.7m long, and weigh up to 340kg with the crew inside. Four-man sleds are up to 3.8m long and, fully loaded, weigh up to 630kg.

Run – a twisting, descending, U-shaped concrete track* covered with artificial ice, with banked turns that allow sleds to run up the sides and make corners without slowing. A full-sized run measures 1,200–1,300m (or up to three-quarters of a mile) long.

Speedsuit – a one-piece, full-length bodysuit worn by sledders to decrease drag.

Helmet – hard plastic headgear similar to a motorcycle helmet. Worn by all sledders to protect the skull in the event that the bobsleigh flips over (which can be very dangerous).

---

* Not unlike those long flume slides you see at water parks. Only it's a half-tube rather than a full tube and is covered with ice.

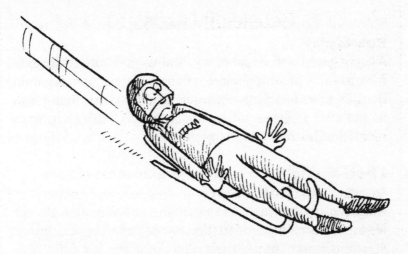

The one-man **skeleton** is different again. Like the luge, it's basically a flat plastic platform with steel runners beneath. But instead of lying on it face-up athletes lie *chest-down* on the skeleton sled's '**saddle**', with their *heads hanging off the front end* and their legs and feet trailing behind.

What? That's crazy! What happens if they crash?

Then they crash face first, finding out rather quickly how good a helmet they're wearing. Again, the skeleton doesn't go as fast as the bobsleigh (or even the luge). But, as skeleton athletes will tell you, 75mph (120km/h) feels like 175mph when you're hurtling down the track *face first*.

I bet! So how do luge and skeleton riders start, stop and steer?

As in bobsleigh, luge and skeletons athletes move their sleds to a starting line at the top of the run, and at the starting signal launch their sleds into the icy run. They launch their sleds, though, in slightly different ways.

Luge racers start *sitting on their luges*, holding on to **starting handles** attached to the track itself. They start with a huge pull, then paddle their hands for extra speed before lying back to steer through the run. Pressing on the steering bows gives them fine control over their turns. But, like bobsledders, luge riders also have to lean and shift their bodies to prevent the luge from flipping over on fast turns.

Skeleton racers start *standing*, holding on to their sleds with both hands. Like bobsledders, they sprint and push their sleds up to speed before leaping on. But unlike bobsledders, they do this face first, *belly-flopping* on to the moving sled. Getting this launch wrong, of course, can have disastrous results. A poorly balanced sledder will either fall off immediately, or be unable to make turns at full speed for fear of flipping the sled.

From this point on, athletes steer and lean their bodies to belt through the run at maximum speed. Luge and skeleton racers **brake** by dropping their heels (on a luge) or toes (on a skeleton) – dragging them on the ice to increase friction. As in bobsleigh, luge and skeleton races are held in heats, and the fastest times win.

OK . . . I *have* to try that one day.
Go for it! Just make sure you buy a decent crash-helmet first . . .

'We had faith we were as great as anybody on the day, and that we could be the best in the world.'

Nicole Minichiello,
British bobsledder and Winter Olympics gold medallist

Luge/Skeleton

How to play
High-speed winter sports in which solo or paired sledders launch themselves on to an ice-covered track, then steer it through banking twists and turns, trying to reach the finish as quickly as possible. The main difference from bobsleigh is that luge and skeleton athletes lie *on top of* a small, steel-runnered sled, rather than sitting within an enclosed craft. Luge racers fly down the track *feet first*, while skeleton racers* go *head first*.

---

* Arguably the bravest – or craziest – of all athletes.

Players

Luge: one or two athletes per sled, competing one at a time, in timed runs.

Skeleton: one athlete per sled, competing one at a time, in timed runs.

Equipment

Luge – a moulded fibreglass seat (a bit like a short ironing board) mounted upon twin steel runners that turn up at the end forming the **steering bows**. Around 1.5m long, and weighing less than 23kg.

Skeleton sled – a 1m-long fibreglass sled with two handles for steering.

Helmet – streamlined version of those used in bobsleigh. Luge helmets are flat, to allow air to stream past the face-up athlete. Skeleton helmets are a bit more elongated from front to back, to help the athlete cut through the air face-first.

Speedsuit – like those used in bobsleigh, only with added reinforcement to protect the spine in the event of a crash.

Afterword

It's all in the training

Elite athletes seem to approach (and even go beyond) the very *limits* of human ability. But in reality, it's all in the *training*, whether it's training the body, or training the mind.

As we learned in chapter 1, elite track and field athletes train their bodies to alter the structure of their muscles, hugely increasing their strength and explosive power.

In chapter 2, we saw how runners, cyclists and cross-country skiers train to alter the oxygen-delivering function of their lungs, hearts and blood vessels, gaining incredible fitness and endurance.

In chapter 3, we saw how archers, basketballers and footballers train their nervous systems to perform complex skills, allowing them to make incredibly accurate shots, curl a ball through the air and more.

And in chapter 4 we saw how gymnasts, divers, surfers and BMX freestylers train their nervous systems to sense and control the movement of their bodies, boards and bikes in mid-air.

So if *they* can do it, why can't *you*? What are you waiting for? *Now get out there and* **train!**

Index

Why is SNOT green?

The First Science Museum Question and Answer Book

Glenn Murphy

Why is snot green? Do rabbits fart? What is space made of? Where does all the water go at low tide? Can animals talk? What are scabs for? Will computers ever be cleverer than people?

Discover the answers to these and an awful lot of other brilliant questions frequently asked at the Science Museum in this wonderfully funny and informative book.

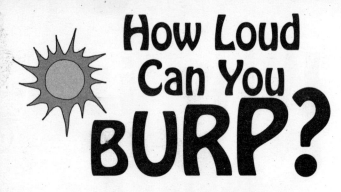

How Loud Can You BURP?

and other extremely important questions (and answers) from the Science Museum

Glenn Murphy

How loud can you burp? Could we use animal poo in power stations to make electricity? Why is water wet, and is anything wetter than water? What's the deadliest disease in the world? What are clouds for?

A second volume of questions and answers from the Science Museum by the author of the mega-bestselling WHY IS SNOT GREEN? A wonderfully funny and informative book with loads of fascinating facts and no boring bits!